Best Easy Day Hikes
Grand Junction and Fruita

Help Us Keep This Guide Up to Date

Every effort has been made by the author and editors to make this guide as accurate and useful as possible. However, many things can change after a guide is published—trails are rerouted, regulations change, facilities come under new management, and so forth.

We welcome your comments concerning your experiences with this guide and how you feel it could be improved and kept up to date. While we may not be able to respond to all comments and suggestions, we'll take them to heart, and we'll also make certain to share them with the author. Please send your comments and suggestions to the following address:

Globe Pequot
Reader Response/Editorial Department
246 Goose Lane
Guilford, CT 06437

Or you may e-mail us at:
editorial@falcon.com

Thanks for your input, and happy hiking!

Best Easy Day Hikes Series

Best Easy Day Hikes
Grand Junction
and Fruita

Bill Haggerty

FALCONGUIDES

GUILFORD, CONNECTICUT
HELENA, MONTANA

FALCONGUIDES®

An imprint of Rowman & Littlefield
Falcon, FalconGuides, and Outfit Your Mind are registered trademarks
of Rowman & Littlefield.

Distributed by NATIONAL BOOK NETWORK

Copyright © 2015 by Rowman & Littlefield
Maps: Hartdale Maps © Rowman & Littlefield

British Library Cataloguing-in-Publication Information available

Library of Congress Cataloging-in-Publication Data available

ISBN 978-1-4930-0977-0 (paperback)
ISBN 978-1-4930-1679-2 (e-book)

♾™ The paper used in this publication meets the minimum require-
ments of American National Standard for Information Sciences—
Permanence of Paper for Printed Library Materials, ANSI/NISO
Z39.48-1992.

Contents

Acknowledgments... vii
Introduction viii
Map Legend.. xiii
Overview Map..xiv

BLM's Bangs Canyon/Tabaguache Area (south of GJ)
1. Mica Mine 2
2. Rough Canyon 5
3. Dominguez Canyon 9

Grand Mesa Forest, Fruita Division (southwest of GJ)
4. Turkey Flats... 15

Colorado National Monument (west of GJ)
5. Echo Canyon 20
6. Devils Kitchen.. 24
7. No Thoroughfare Canyon 28
8. Serpents Trail... 33
9. Liberty Cap/Corkscrew Loop 36
10. Coke Ovens 40
11. Monument Canyon.. 43

Adjacent to Colorado National Monument in Grand Junction and Fruita
12. Riggs Hill 48
13. Dinosaur Hill... 52

McInnis Canyons National Conservation Area (front country northwest of GJ)
14. Kodels Canyon 57
15. Devils Canyon.. 61

16. Fruita Paleontological Area 65
17. Pollock Bench 68

McInnis Canyons/Blackridge Wilderness Area (backcountry northwest of GJ)

18. Rattlesnake Canyon Arches Loop 74
19. Mee Canyon.. 78

BLM Rabbit Valley (west of GJ)

20. McDonald Creek Cultural Area... 83
21. Trail Through Time... 86

BLM Book Cliffs Area (northeast of GJ)

22. Coal Canyon 91

Grand Mesa National Forest (east of GJ)

23. West Bench 96
24. Crag Crest 101
25. Lake of the Woods 106

Colorado River (through the center of the Grand Valley)

26. Colorado Riverfront Trail 111

Appendix 118
About the Author.. 119

Acknowledgments

"'Tis a privilege to live in Colorado," my dearly departed mother would say. Dad took us camping, fishing, and hiking to prove her point. Thanks, Mom and Dad, for instilling in me that appreciation of Colorado's spectacular natural resources.

To the love of my life, my wife Glenda, and children, Bridgette and Austin, thank you for supporting me, hiking with me, and allowing me to write, hike, bike, fish, ski, explore, and live life fully here in western Colorado.

Special thanks to hiking/biking/skiing companion Nick Massaro, and to Steven Marshall, a fabulous artist and good friend who accompanied me on many of these hikes.

Thanks to my former colleagues at the Colorado Division of Wildlife (now called Parks and Wildlife) for being dear friends and great mentors.

Thanks to all the hard-working public servants of the Colorado National Monument, Bureau of Land Management, and USDA Forest Service. You are true stewards of our land and your work is very much underappreciated. Special thanks to my reviewers, John "JT" Toolen, Collin Ewing, Katie Stevens, Troy Schnurr and Chris Pipkin.

Thank you Larry Seidl for introducing me to Falcon, and thank you Steve Culpepper and all the fine editors at Rowman & Littlefield for your precise editing and for making this project happen.

Most importantly, thank you, dear readers. Happy Trails!

Introduction

"This is a tough job." That's what I thought as I crawled through a window arch carved into solid rock by the forces of wind and water over millions of years. I snapped a photo on the opposite side of the arch, above a Navajo-style ladder propped against the yellow and rust-colored sandstone ledge and gazed into the depths of the Black Ridge Wilderness Area. Mesmerized by the beauty of the upper Colorado Plateau, I climbed down the stout ladder and into an immense alcove along a path used by native tribes 1,000 years ago.

I was less than 25 miles from town, yet there was no one else on this trail. The silence was deafening.

I then meandered through a field of multicolored wildflowers on my way to the crest of the Grand Mesa—the largest flattop mountain in the Northern Hemisphere—just to ensure my GPS coordinates were correct.

That was tough.

I peered through a kaleidoscopic maze of spires, hoodoos, and canyons where wild horses roam in the awe-inspiring Book Cliffs, all to ensure the accuracy of this guide.

I wandered beneath giant sandstone monoliths with names like Independence Monument, Kissing Couple, and Coke Ovens in a national monument only minutes from my home—all in hot pursuit of journalistic excellence.

I felt the pulse of the Colorado River on a gentle voyage through Grand Junction, named for the two largest rivers in the state, the Colorado (formerly called Grand River) and the Gunnison, which converge here.

Tough job, but someone had to do it!

Grand Junction and Fruita sit in spectacular country—the Colorado Grand Valley, a 30-mile stretch of land alongside the Colorado River that is rugged yet gentle, remote yet close to home, vibrant yet subtle with contrast.

The remarkable Colorado National Monument, operated by the National Park Service, borders the southwest edge of the valley, while the Bureau of Land Management's Dominguez-Escalante National Conservation Area and Dominguez Canyon Wilderness Area lie directly south.

BLM's McInnis Canyons National Conservation Area—including the Black Ridge Wilderness Area—is situated to the west. The 10,000-foot-high Grand Mesa within the national forest that is its namesake looms over the valley to the east, while Mount Garfield and the unique Book Cliffs range define the valley's north and northeastern flank.

This variegated maze of canyons and mountains, the breadth of the valley, the gentle roar of the river, and the incredible and diverse recreational opportunities all draw outdoor enthusiasts to the Grand Valley.

Of course, a world-class fruit and wine industry is worth the trip all by itself. Our climate, topography, and geology—and the Colorado River—create perfect conditions for orchardists and vintners. Those same conditions, and that same river, allow the rest of us to play outside year-round.

Through eons of time, the Colorado River created and defined the Grand Valley and much of the geologic splendor you'll see here on the Colorado Plateau. The Colorado is not the same as it was when it carved the Grand Canyon. It has been dammed and tamed in order to serve some thirty million people who now occupy Colorado and six downstream US states, as well as Mexico.

Nonetheless, it remains the lifeblood of the Grand Valley and the entire desert Southwest. Because of its impact on the geology, geography, and history of the area, the Colorado River also plays an integral part in this guide's collection of the area's twenty-six best hikes.

Are they all easy hikes? That's for you to decide. I think they're easy, but I am well acclimated to this altitude. Plus, I spend so much time pausing to look up at the huge western sky, or across the valley at grazing desert bighorn sheep, or down at a delicate desert wildflower through the lens of my camera—that I rarely break a sweat.

If you study the overview map, you'll notice a couple of gaps in this 360-degree tour of the valley. That's because some of the hikes around here are tough. Really tough. Like Mount Garfield, that behemoth of a dirt pile on the north as you enter the Grand Valley at Palisade. My son affectionately calls the hike up Mount Garfield "a death march." It's not included here.

Also not included is a fabulous yet strenuous hike up Tellerico Trail leading to a band of wild horses along the top of the Book Cliffs north of Fruita. Nor is upper No Thoroughfare Canyon. It's only 5 miles from the center of Grand Junction, but it's a gnarly backcountry hike on a trail that could only be labeled "primitive" at best.

No, this is a collection of hikes for all of us, the old and the young, the bold and the cautious, avid hikers and occasional wanderers. It's not for those who don't like fresh air. It's not for those whose shoes fall apart when they leave pavement (although the Colorado Riverfront Trail is paved!).

There are a few things to remember about hiking around here. First, the weather is usually great. The Grand Valley experiences an average of 310 days of sun each year. Even on those rare cloudy days, you can still enjoy the outdoors. However, this is still Colorado, and the weather can change in a matter of minutes, so be prepared. A half inch of rain can cause flash floods in desert canyons. In the mountains, a sudden snowstorm can leave you stranded and cold, even hypothermic.

Summertime temperatures can easily reach into the 100s in the valley. That's a good time to stick by the river or head to the high country. Choose to hike in the early morning or late evening if you hike in the desert in the summer.

At all times of year, carry extra water. Experts suggest a gallon per day per person in our dry climate. Most of these hikes won't take you a full day, but rather a couple hours. At the very least, drink lots of water before you go, then carry a couple extra quarts of water with you.

In the winter, the Grand Mesa under 8 feet of snow creates a wonderland for cross-country skiers. It's no place for hikers, though, unless you have snowshoes. That's the time to visit the desert.

Any time of year you travel to the Grand Mesa, remember it's nearly 2 miles above sea level. Acclimate slowly and drink lots of water. If you get a nasty headache or you're feeling dizzy, retreat to a lower elevation immediately. Altitude sickness can be deadly. Again, weather can change abruptly, so be prepared with hat, gloves, warm gear, and fire-starting tools, even during the summer.

Early spring is mud season around here. Be careful where you hike. Desert soils are fragile and erode easily. These soils, when wet, will suck the boot right off your foot.

Always remember, wildlife is everywhere and this is their home. Please treat both wildlife and their habitat with respect. Keep your dogs on leashes in areas where desert bighorn sheep may be lambing. Don't let them chase the mule deer found from the river bottom to the top of Grand Mesa.

Watch out for others, especially along the Colorado Riverfront Trail. It gets lots of use by bicyclists, dog walkers, in-line skaters, and mothers with strollers. Courtesy and caution are encouraged.

Throughout this arid country, please tread lightly. Take only pictures, leave only footprints.

A local legend maintains that if you put a little dirt in your pocket when you leave the Grand Valley, you're bound to return. I hope you find these hikes so enjoyable that you stick a little dirt in your pocket and return often to enjoy this outdoor wonderland.

Happy Trails!
Bill

Map Legend

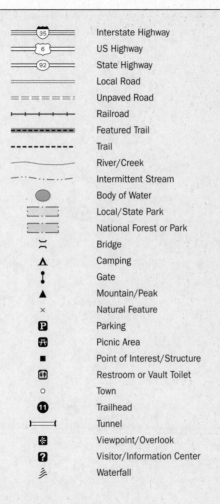	

Interstate Highway

US Highway

State Highway

Local Road

Unpaved Road

Railroad

Featured Trail

Trail

River/Creek

Intermittent Stream

Body of Water

Local/State Park

National Forest or Park

Bridge

Camping

Gate

Mountain/Peak

Natural Feature

Parking

Picnic Area

Point of Interest/Structure

Restroom or Vault Toilet

Town

Trailhead

Tunnel

Viewpoint/Overlook

Visitor/Information Center

Waterfall

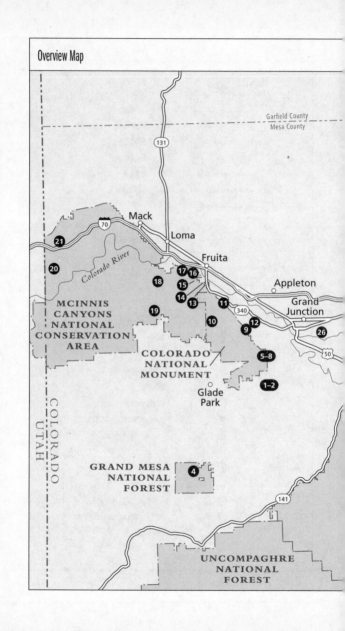

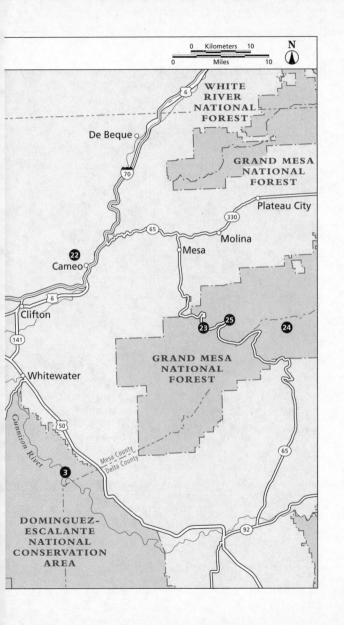

BLM's Bangs Canyon/ Tabaguache Area (south of GJ)

1 Mica Mine

Mica glitters brightly in the BLM's Bangs Canyon area, located at an elevation of 6,155 feet and only 8.2 miles from the corner of Fourth and Main Streets in Grand Junction. The word "mica" comes from the Latin *micare*, meaning "to glitter," in reference to the brilliant appearance of the mineral that was once mined here in the 1950s. Mica is a component of numerous products, including electrical insulation and windows.

Distance: 2.8 miles out and back

Hiking time: About 1 to 2 hours

Difficulty: Easy; great hike for kids; not wheelchair accessible

Trail surface: Old double-track dirt road at start of trail, then sandstone rock and dirt

Best season: Good year-round, but very hot in the middle of summer

Other trail users: Foot travel only

Canine compatibility: Dogs allowed if under control; owners required to pick up after pets

Maps: USGS Island Mesa, BLM Grand Junction Resource Area, Third Flats Shared Trails, Bangs Canyon (brochure)

Trail contact: BLM Grand Junction Field Office, 2815 H Rd., Grand Junction, CO 81506; (970) 244-3000, blm.gov/co/st/en/fo/gjfo.html

Finding the trailhead: Take Broadway across the Grand Avenue Bridge (CO 340) and turn left onto Monument Road. Turn left again in one-quarter mile onto D Road. In 1 mile, D Road takes a hard right turn and becomes Rosevale Road. In another mile, turn right onto Little Park Road. Continue for 6 miles to the BLM's Bangs Canyon Staging Area (approximately 3 miles past the Little Park Trailhead) and park here. The trailhead is located next to the BLM map and signs on the kiosk. GPS: N38 59.3218' / W108 37.0570'

The Hike

This is a short, fun jaunt for the whole family. It starts from the parking lot to the right of the BLM's informational kiosks and immediately descends through a large cut in the sandstone. At 0.2 mile, the trail splits. To the left is Rough Canyon; to the right is Mica Mine Trail. Turn right and meander beneath the large Fremont cottonwood trees, then follow the streambed and a well-used dirt trail that bobs from side to side alongside it traveling southwest. In about a mile, you'll begin to see lots of fine white quartz along the trail and on a bench to your left—a byproduct of mining for mica and decorative landscape quartz. In 1.4 miles, as you round the next bend, watch for another short trail to your left through the willows. Take that trail to the left and walk a hundred feet to the shallow, open-faced mine. It's very safe.

Mica is the only mineral that can be bent without breaking. That is because it can be peeled into very thin sheets, as you'll see scattered throughout this area. BLM requests that you leave the mica here and take only pictures!

Continuing on the main trail leads hikers into Ladder Canyon and a much more extensive wilderness trek. The Ladder Canyon Trail is also accessible from the Lunch Loop/Tabaguache Trailhead on Monument Road leading into the Colorado National Monument from Grand Junction.

Miles and Directions

0.0 Start from trailhead at Bangs Canyon Staging Area.

0.2 At the confluence with Rough Canyon Trail, turn right.

0.5 Begin to see glitter on the trail.

1.0 Cross the creek bed.

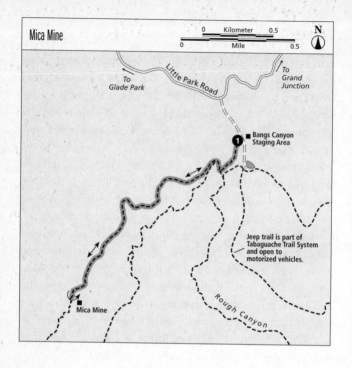

Mica Mine

0   Kilometer   0.5
0   Mile   0.5

N

To Glade Park

Little Park Road

To Grand Junction

1 Bangs Canyon Staging Area

Jeep trail is part of Tabaguache Trail System and open to motorized vehicles.

Rough Canyon

Mica Mine

1.1 Ground white quartz looks like white sand on the trail.

1.3 The sandstone canyon gives way to hard granite.

1.4 Turn left on narrow trail through willows and hike 100 feet to explore this open-faced mine. Turn back here.

2.8 Arrive back at trailhead.

2 Rough Canyon

Rough Canyon, only 8.6 miles from downtown Grand Junction, is geologically fascinating and home to some of the world's rarest plants and animals. As its name implies, it's also rough, rugged, and rocky. Well, it's rugged, but not that rough. You can't make it down with a walker, but you don't need ropes either.

Distance: 4.5-mile loop

Hiking time: About 2 to 3 hours

Difficulty: Moderate

Trail surface: Rough backcountry route

Best season: Year-round, but very hot in the summer

Other trail users: Foot traffic only on the way to Rough Canyon Falls; ATVs, four-wheel-drive vehicles, mountain bikers, and horseback riders on the way back

Canine compatibility: Dogs allowed if under control

Fees and permits: None

Maps: USGS Island Mesa; Trails Illustrated Colorado National Monument/McInnis Canyons NCA; BLM Grand Junction Resource Area, Third Flats Shared Trails, Bangs Canyon (brochure)

Trail contacts: BLM Grand Junction Field Office, 2815 H Rd., Grand Junction, CO 81506; (970) 244-3000, blm.gov/co/st/en/fo/gjfo.html

Special considerations: Some trail-finding skills may be required in this canyon as the trail is not well-traveled.

Finding the trailhead: Take Broadway across the Grand Avenue Bridge (CO 340) and turn left onto Monument Road. Turn left again in one-quarter mile onto D Road. In 1 mile, D Road takes a hard right turn and becomes Rosevale Road. In another mile, turn right onto Little Park Road. Continue for 6 miles to the BLM's Bangs Canyon Staging Area (approximately 3 miles past the Little Park Trailhead) and park here. The trailhead is located next to the BLM map and signs on the kiosk. GPS: N38 59.3218' / W108 37.0570'

The Hike

The best time of year to visit this little-used trail is mid- to late May when the wildflowers are in full bloom—orange desert globemallow, flowering cliffrose, pink and yellow prickly pear cactus, vibrant-red claret cup cactus, burnt-red Indian paintbrush, hairy goldenaster, purple desert lupine—right here in the desert only minutes from downtown Grand Junction.

It gets extremely hot in the middle of summer, yet early in the morning and late in the evening, this trail offers an enjoyable, if not aerobic, hike. In the springtime, with water still flowing steadily through this canyon, it's cool and shady for much of the day.

Hikers, jeeps, ATVs, horses, motorcycles, and bicycles share many of the trails in this special management area, but the hiking trails to both Rough Canyon Falls and the Mica Mine are for foot traffic only. Motorized vehicles and bicycles are not allowed. You'll see why after 125 yards.

The trailhead is well marked, and initially the trail leads to both the Mica Mine and Rough Canyon. It splits in 0.2 mile. The right fork takes you to the Mica Mine, while the left trail leads to the tangled maze of Rough Canyon, where the spineless hedgehog cactus and rare canyon tree frog live.

You may or may not spot either of these, since they are rare. You might up your chances of spotting the canyon tree frog, though, if you hike in the early morning or late evening from May to September. The little suckers are small—usually about 2.25 inches (57 mm) long, or less—but you can hear them from miles away.

Once you reach Rough Canyon Falls, you can hike back the way you came, or you can find your way to a somewhat

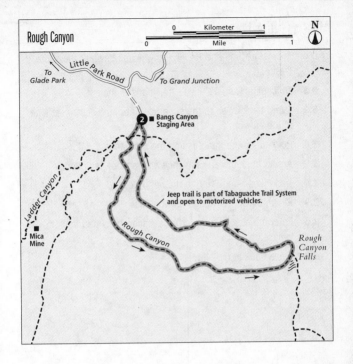

To
Glade Park

Little Park Road

To Grand Junction

2 ■ Bangs Canyon
Staging Area

Jeep trail is part of Tabeguache Trail System
and open to motorized vehicles.

Ladder Canyon

Rough Canyon

■ Mica
Mine

Rough
Canyon
Falls

primitive trail to the left (north) and follow that for a few hundred yards to a parking and four-wheel-drive staging area. This is part of the Tabeguache Trail that leads from Grand Junction to Montrose, 65 miles to the south.

Follow the road leading from this parking area to the north and west, back to your vehicle. The trail is well marked and utilized by ATVs, jeeps, horseback riders, and other hikers, but it's rare that you'll see anyone else in this rough canyon.

Miles and Directions

0.0 Mica Mine Trail and Rough Canyon Trail begin at the same trailhead.

0.2 Trail splits; Rough Canyon Trail leads to the left.

0.9 Climb back down to the streambed from the southwest side of the canyon.

1.0 Rugged granite intrudes into the sandstone.

1.2 An old truck tire and rim show the force of flash floods.

1.5 Trail takes a hard turn to the north (left).

2.3 Reach the top of Rough Canyon Falls.

2.5 Enter the staging area for Tabeguache Trail/road back to vehicle.

5.0 Arrive back at trailhead.

3 Dominguez Canyon

The Dominguez Canyon Wilderness is a 66,280-acre expanse located in the heart of the 210,000-acre Dominguez-Escalante National Conservation Area. Both were created by an act of Congress in 2009. Here, red-rock canyons and sandstone bluffs provide breathtaking scenery and hold geological and paleontological resources spanning 600 million years. This area contains many well-preserved cultural and historical sites from the past 10,000 years, including Newspaper Rock, the destination of this hike. This massive stone bears Ute petroglyphs depicting some of the wildlife you might catch sight of here.

Distance: 6.6 miles out and back

Hiking time: About 2.5 to 4 hours

Difficulty: Easy

Trail surface: Road base for first mile, then wide, smooth dirt path

Best season: Year-round, but very hot during the summer

Other trail users: Foot and horseback travel only; no motorized vehicles, chainsaws, generators, bicycles, or hang gliders

Canine compatibility: Dogs allowed under control and on leash around other users and during spring (lambing season for desert bighorn sheep); owners required to pick up after pets

Fees and permits: None

Maps: USGS Triangle Mesa; BLM Delta Resource Area; USDA Forest Service Uncompahgre National Forest

Trail contacts: BLM Grand Junction Field Office, 2815 H Rd., Grand Junction, CO 81506; (970) 244-3000, blm.gov/co/st/en/nca/denca.html

Finding the trailhead: From Grand Junction, take US 50 south 17 miles past the Mesa County Fairgrounds to Bridgeport Road. (Slow down as you approach the road at the top of the hill, as there is no exit lane.) Turn right on Bridgeport Road and travel down this narrow, well-maintained gravel road for 3 miles to its terminus at the Gunnison River. (Go slowly around single-lane blind corners.) On the left, you will see a new trailhead recently constructed by the BLM. This is the start of a future trail that will be constructed to avoid the railroad tracks. For now, keep travelling to the trailhead near the railroad tracks. GPS: N38 50.9614' / W108 22.3554'

The Hike

This hike doesn't offer scenic views right away. The first mile follows the Denver and Rio Grande Western Railroad tracks and the Gunnison River. While the river is beautiful, it's hidden behind tall stands of tamarisk, rabbitbrush, and greasewood. Be careful as trains stop here regularly. Please do not attempt to cross between train cars.

In about a mile, though, the trip gets interesting! A few hundred feet past an old, closed private bridge, you'll reach a newer pedestrian/horse bridge spanning the river. Cross this bridge and continue traveling upstream, or south.

In 0.3 mile, pass the first of a handful of group camping sites for those floating down the Gunnison River from Delta. Continue past the camping areas along the river for another 0.4 mile until reaching the mouth of Dominguez Canyon. The trail then turns to the west and away from the river. There is a large BLM kiosk and fence marking the wilderness boundary.

The trail here is wide and easy to follow in a southerly direction. In another 0.7 mile, the main trail bends toward the west (right) again as the canyon splits. To the right (west) is Big Dominguez Canyon; to the left (further south) is Little Dominguez Canyon, also within the wilderness area. Continue right for another 0.4 mile and cross through an

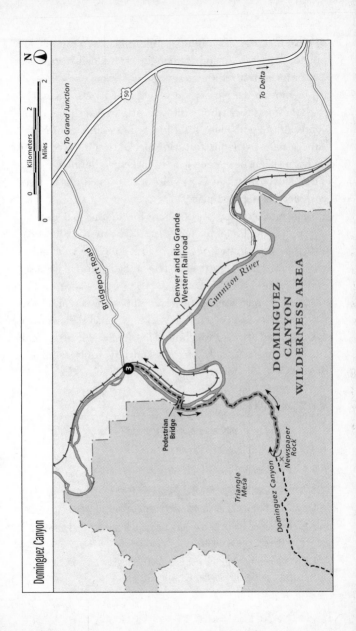

Dominguez Canyon

old livestock fence. Within 0.4 mile, hike past a rock shelter, put to good use during infrequent yet sudden storms that can occur in this region at any time of year.

In another tenth of a mile, Newspaper Rock, a freestanding sandstone rock about the size of a trailer, squats in the center of the trail. Here you can see fine examples of Native American petroglyphs featuring pecked outlines of desert bighorn sheep, bear, deer, lizards, snakes, and human figures. The Native American Utes who once roamed this area still consider this a sacred place.

The trail continues from here for another 6.3 miles to the top of the Uncompahgre Plateau at about 7,500 feet in elevation. (Elevation at the trailhead is 4,682 ft.) To continue would make this a great hike, but probably not a "best easy day hike."

Look up and around, however, as petroglyphs and other Native American artifacts like wickiups (small shelters made of brush) and arrowheads abound in this area. Please remember, however, take only pictures and leave only footprints, then trace your footsteps back to your vehicle.

Miles and Directions

0.0 Start from trailhead along the railroad tracks.

0.3 Road/trail crosses railroad tracks.

0.9 Hike past old black bridge over Gunnison River.

1.0 Cross pedestrian/horse bridge over river.

1.3 Pass first group campground used for river runners.

1.7 Reach mouth of Dominguez Canyon. Stay right and travel into wilderness area.

2.4 Canyon forks; to the left is Little Dominguez Canyon, to the right is Big Dominguez Canyon. Stay right.

2.8 Pass old cattle fence.

3.2 Pass rock shelter.

3.3 Reach Newspaper Rock; retrace your steps from here.

6.6 Arrive back at trailhead.

Grand Mesa Forest, Fruita Division (southwest of GJ)

4 Turkey Flats

A small section of public land on Glade Park above the Colorado National Monument is managed by the Grand Mesa National Forest. It's situated in a beautiful aspen grove at 8,400 feet in elevation and it's a great place to escape the summer heat in the Grand Valley below.

Distance: 5.3-mile loop
Hiking time: About 2 to 3 hours
Difficulty: Easy (moderate if altitude is an issue)
Trail surface: Narrow backcountry path most of the way—gravel road for part of trip back to vehicle
Best season: Spring, summer, early fall
Other trail users: Mountain bikers, horseback riders
Canine compatibility: Dogs allowed if under control
Fees and permits: None
Maps: USDA Forest Service Grand Mesa National Forest; USGS Fish Creek and Snyder Flats
Trail contacts: Grand Mesa National Forest, Grand Valley District, 2777 Crossroads Blvd., Grand Junction, CO 81506; (970) 242-8211, fs.usda.gov/contactus/gmug/about-forest/contactus
Other: This is a popular place during the fall big-game hunting seasons (main rifle seasons are from mid-Oct to mid-Nov). At this time of year, it's better to stick to trails within the Colorado National Monument where no hunting is allowed.

Finding the trailhead: Take Monument Road to the east entrance of the Colorado National Monument. (You don't have to pay the park fee if you're going to Glade Park.) Once you're through the tunnel and pass Cold Shivers Point, turn left at the Glade Park turnoff. Travel to the Glade Park Store, then turn left onto 16.5 Road. The pavement ends in another 2.6 miles. Stay on this well-maintained dirt road, but watch your speed around a few blind curves. Mud Springs Campground is

4.2 miles past the end of the pavement. In another 1.3 miles, take the right fork toward the Fruita Division of the Grand Mesa National Forest. In 1.5 miles you'll enter forest property as 16.5 Road becomes FR 400. Travel past the turnoff to Fruita Reservoir No.1 and the Fruita Picnic Grounds (FR 400 2C), then past Fruita Reservoir No. 2. About 0.3 mile past Reservoir No. 2, you'll see the Turkey Flats Trailhead on your left. Park on the right. GPS: N38 51.7342' / W108 46.3585'

The Hike

This trail begins with a small climb through a lush aspen forest before angling through a transition zone of aspen and spruce. Wildflowers are abundant throughout this area for most of the late spring and summer. All along this trail, you should see elk prints and deer track. You may also stumble upon a blue grouse or wild turkey.

In 1.3 miles, you'll top out at 9,203 feet, and then meander down into a long, lovely park where the Turkey Flats trail meets Haypress Trail (No. 662). Go left or south and continue on the Turkey Flats Trail (No. 661) through another beautiful grove of aspen. You'll climb and drop in elevation for a little more than a mile before you drop into a gully with a couple of stripped trail markers. Continue forward and to the left on the most-used trail here and eventually you'll find yourself on the dirt road that leads to Fruita Reservoir No. 1 (to the right) and the Fruita Picnic Grounds (to your left), which you passed on your drive to the trailhead.

Here, you can either turn around and follow your own tracks back to the vehicle, or complete the loop by turning left and following the road past the picnic grounds, then left again on the main dirt road back to the trailhead. It is 1.9 miles down the dirt roads back to the vehicle, but it will allow you to actually see what you passed on your way in.

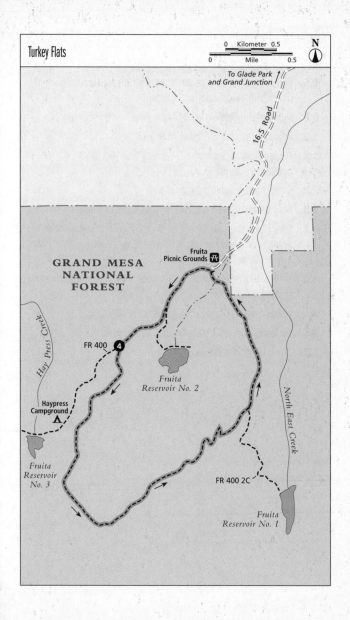

Turkey Flats

0   Kilometer 0.5
0   Mile   0.5

N

To Glade Park
and Grand Junction

16.5 Road

GRAND MESA
NATIONAL
FOREST

Fruita
Picnic Grounds

Hay Press Creek

FR 400   4

Haypress
Campground

Fruita
Reservoir No. 2

Fruita
Reservoir
No. 3

FR 400 2C

North East Creek

Fruita
Reservoir
No. 1

Miles and Directions

0.0 Start from Turkey Flats Trailhead on FR 400.

0.5 Top your climb to a bench meadow on your left (southeast), beneath a steep wooded hillside.

0.9 Proceed through old, out-of-use gate.

1.3 Reach peak trail elevation of 9,203 feet.

1.4 Turkey Flats Trail crosses Haypress Trail (No. 662). Go left, continuing south.

2.2 Descend through long grassy valley.

2.9 Stay on main path marked by stripped trail marker.

3.1 Hike down the switchback to the bottom of the gully and another stripped trail sign. Keep left as the trail splits. (Path forward is being rehabilitated.)

3.2 Your detour is rewarded with a cool rock structure adjacent to the path.

3.6 Turkey Flats Trail (No. 661) meets FR 400 2C.

4.5 FR Road 400 2C meets FR 400 at Fruita Picnic Grounds.

5.3 Arrive back at trailhead.

Colorado National Monument (west of GJ)

5 Echo Canyon

This trail ends in a box canyon where a 100-foot waterfall spills intermittently, leaving streaks of minerals and water on the sandstone cliffs and a large pool at the base of the waterfall that provides nourishment to 200-year-old Freemont cottonwoods.

Distance: 2.8 miles out and back

Hiking time: About 1 to 2 hours

Difficulty: Easy to moderate

Trail surface: Rocky backcountry surface

Best season: Year-round

Other trail users: Foot travel only

Canine compatibility: No dogs allowed

Fees and permits: Weekly pass needed; annual pass available; national parks pass OK for admission

Maps: USGS Colorado National Monument; Trails Illustrated Colorado National Monument/McInnis Canyons NCA

Trail contacts: Colorado National Monument, Fruita, CO 81521; (970) 858-3616, nps .gov/colm

Other: Guided walks given weekly during spring, summer, and fall

Finding the trailhead: This trailhead is located just inside the east entrance of the Colorado National Monument on Monument Road (turn left onto Monument Road off Broadway after it crosses the Colorado River and proceed 3.3 miles). From the entrance gate, travel 0.2 mile. Park on the left. (***Note:*** This is also the parking area for Old Gordon Trail, No Thoroughfare Canyon, Devils Kitchen, and Serpents Trail. If this parking area is full, park across the road at the Devils Kitchen picnic area.) GPS: N39 01.9064' / W108 37.8414'

The Hike

The Echo Canyon Trail offers a short, mostly gentle hike that follows the canyon bottom to its boxed end. One stretch climbs about 300 feet in elevation on very solid rock, but other than that, it's pretty easy.

This scenery is similar to many canyons within the Colorado National Monument—same rock, same rock formation. Even the waterfall at the boxed end of Echo Canyon, about a mile and a half from the parking lot, looks quite similar to the "first waterfall" described in the No Thoroughfare Canyon hike (hike No 7. in this guide). However, Echo Canyon, the most southern canyon within the national monument, is quite unique. It ends in this boxed canyon, while the much longer No Thoroughfare Canyon to the north continues to the top of the Colorado National Monument.

Echo Canyon is one of the few places in Colorado where you can search for canyon treefrogs. These unique amphibians are found from the southwestern United States through central Mexico. In Colorado, however, they exist only along the south rim of the Colorado River west of Grand Junction and in John Brown Canyon near Gateway, Colorado, along the Utah border.

Treefrogs are tiny suckers—they could hide in the palm of your hand. Yet, a treefrog's call is loud, described as "the bleat of a goat or a hoarse sheep" in Geoffrey Hammerson's *Amphibians and Reptiles in Colorado*.

Canyon treefrogs don't climb trees. Rather, they retreat to rock crevices in hot weather and during the cold season. Most activity occurs from May to September along small bodies of water in Echo Canyon, and that's the best time to visit, especially early in the morning and late in the evening.

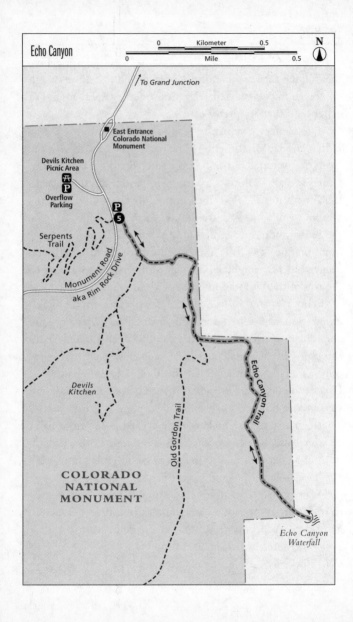

Echo Canyon

0   Kilometer   0.5

0   Mile   0.5

N

To Grand Junction

East Entrance
Colorado National
Monument

Devils Kitchen
Picnic Area

Overflow
Parking

Serpents
Trail

Monument Road
aka Rim Rock Drive

Devils
Kitchen

Old Gordon Trail

Echo Canyon Trail

COLORADO
NATIONAL
MONUMENT

Echo Canyon
Waterfall

That's the time of day when you're most likely to hear or see the canyon treefrog. It's also the best time of the day to watch the shadows and colors change in this short, yet spectacular canyon.

Miles and Directions

0.0   Start from trailhead on Monument Road/Rim Rock Drive.

0.1   Trail splits. Stay to the left and follow signs to Echo Canyon Trail/Old Gordon Trail.

0.3   Trail crosses creek bottom.

0.6   Trail splits—to the right is Old Gordon Trail. Continue forward along Echo Canyon Trail and follow signs.

0.7   Ten steps lead down toward the canyon.

1.0   If there's water in the canyon, it will pool here.

1.4   Reach your destination: the boxed end of the canyon and the waterfall.

2.8   Arrive back at trailhead.

6 Devils Kitchen

Devils Kitchen is a great place for the entire family to play. A short out-and-back hike makes this an easy, quick way to explore the fascinating geology of the Colorado National Monument.

Distance: 1.2 miles out and back
Hiking time: About 45 minutes
Difficulty: Easy—some elevation gain as you enter the "kitchen"
Trail surface: Mostly smooth, hard sand and dirt. Steps carved in stone are found part of the way.
Best season: Year-round
Other trail users: Foot traffic only
Canine compatibility: No dogs allowed

Fees and permits: 7-day permits for hikers/bikers or cars; yearly monument pass or national parks pass also usable
Maps: USGS Colorado National Monument; Trails Illustrated Colorado National Monument/McInnis Canyons NCA
Trail contacts: Colorado National Monument, Fruita, CO 81521; (970) 858-3616, nps .gov/colm
Other: Elevation ranges—4,944 to 5,173 feet; guided walks available except in winter

Finding the trailhead: This trailhead is located just inside the east entrance of the Colorado National Monument on Monument Road (turn left off Broadway after it crosses the Colorado River and proceed 3.3 miles). From the entrance gate, travel 0.2 mile. Park on the left. (*Note:* This is also the parking area for Old Gordon Trail, No Thoroughfare Canyon, Echo Canyon, and Serpents Trail. If this parking area is full, park across the road in the Devils Kitchen picnic area.) GPS: N39 01.9025' / W108 37.8484'

The Hike

Devils Kitchen Trail is a short out-and-back hike that will introduce you to the interesting geology and formations of the Colorado National Monument. The "kitchen" is simply a natural opening formed by a circle of huge upright sandstone boulders. The well-marked trail to Devils Kitchen is relatively gentle, but there is 229 feet of ascent as you climb among the freestanding monoliths of this area.

The trailhead at the south end of the parking area is also the trailhead for No Thoroughfare Canyon, Echo Canyon, and Old Gordon Trail. Follow the joint trails for 0.2 mile to the first fork. Adhering to the instructional signs, take the right fork. The trail splits again in another tenth of a mile. This time, take the left fork and cross over the creek bed, again following the signs pointing toward Devils Kitchen.

Soon, you'll climb a set of stone steps. The trail is easy to follow to this point. Beyond these steps, you'll discover the first of many rock cairns, piles of rock serving as markers, which here point the way to Devils Kitchen. Many social trails exist in this area, so stay on the established trail and follow the carved steps up the slickrock. As you approach the base of the rock formation, you can either scramble up and stand among the giants or go left around it and hike into the rock opening.

These free-standing boulders are composed of Wingate sandstone capped by a thin remnant of the erosion-resistant Kayenta Formation.

Be careful playing in the Kitchen, especially when it's wet, as this slickrock comes by its name naturally!

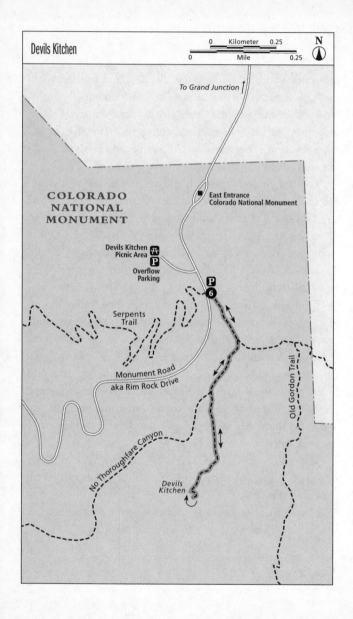

Devils Kitchen

0 Kilometer 0.25
0 Mile 0.25

N

To Grand Junction

■ East Entrance
Colorado National Monument

COLORADO
NATIONAL
MONUMENT

Devils Kitchen
Picnic Area

Overflow
Parking

P
6

Serpents
Trail

Monument Road
aka Rim Rock Drive

Old Gordon Trail

No Thoroughfare Canyon

*Devils
Kitchen*

Miles and Directions

0.0 Start from trailhead at south end of parking area.

0.2 Trail forks; take right fork and follow signs.

0.3 Trail splits again; take left fork and cross over dry creek bed.

0.4 The short climb to the "kitchen" begins by climbing a set of stone steps.

0.5 Reach the first of many rock cairns, piles of rock that mark the trail from here to the top.

0.6 Stand beneath the giant stone pillars in the Devils Kitchen.

1.2 Arrive back at trailhead.

7 No Thoroughfare Canyon

No Thoroughfare Canyon is wild and deep, exposing gray-black Precambrian metamorphic rock that is 1.7 billion years old—some of the oldest on the Colorado Plateau. A one-way hike from top to bottom is 8.5 miles and difficult. Backcountry pathfinding skills are necessary. However, a great 2-mile hike delivers you to an impressive intermittent waterfall. Another aerobic 1-mile hike beyond that takes you to a second waterfall dwarfing the first. You can then hike back the way you came.

Distance: 4 miles out and back to first waterfall; 6 miles out and back to second waterfall

Hiking time: About 2 to 4 hours

Difficulty: Easy to first waterfall, moderate to difficult to second waterfall

Trail surface: Easy wide path to start, then a narrow but well-worn backcountry path to the first waterfall; primitive backcountry trail beyond that

Best season: Year-round

Other trail users: Foot travel only

Canine compatibility: No dogs allowed

Fees and permits: 7-day permits for hikers/bikers or cars; yearly monument pass or national parks pass also usable

Maps: USGS Colorado National Monument; Trails Illustrated Colorado National Monument/McInnis Canyons NCA

Trail contacts: Colorado National Monument, Fruita, CO 81521; (970) 858-3616, nps.gov/colm

Special considerations: This area gets very hot in the summer. Take plenty of extra water, sunscreen, a hat, and sunglasses. Gnats can also be a problem during the heat of the summer, so come prepared with your favorite insect repellant. The little water you'll find here is not drinkable, but please don't pollute because this water is home to the rare canyon treefrog, red-spotted toad, and Woodhouse's toad and provides life and nourishment to numerous other species of wildlife.

Other: Guided walks available except in winter

Finding the trailhead: The lower No Thoroughfare Canyon trailhead is located just inside the east entrance of the Colorado National Monument on Monument Road. Take Grand Avenue across the Colorado River and turn left at the first light, Monument Road. Proceed 3.3 miles to the east entrance of the monument. Travel another 0.2 mile. Park on the left. (**Note:** This is also the parking area for Serpents Trail, Old Gordon Trail, Devils Kitchen, and Echo Canyon. If this parking area is full, park across the road in the Devils Kitchen picnic area.) GPS: N39 01.0479' / W108 38.9724'

The Hike

No Thoroughfare Canyon Trail is one of the longest and most primitive hiking trails in the monument. The lower 2 miles, however, are well used, and the spills and waterfalls, although intermittent, are picturesque and provide an oasis in the desert. The gray-black Precambrian metamorphic rocks found here are colorfully overlaid by sedimentary rock layers. Those layers are composed of clay and silt deposited by water and wind during the Mesozoic Era, from 160 to 225 million years ago.

The trail starts at the south end of the parking area and forks twice within 0.3 mile. Follow the directional signs to the right both times. Within a mile, you'll come to the first pool. This is a large pour-off created through eons of flash floods, siltation, searing heat, wind, and water erosion, yet it is considered slight compared to the waterfalls ahead.

Continue upstream by taking the eighty steep steps to the right of the pool, then dropping back into the creek bottom. Travel another 0.9 mile to the first waterfall, where you'll find

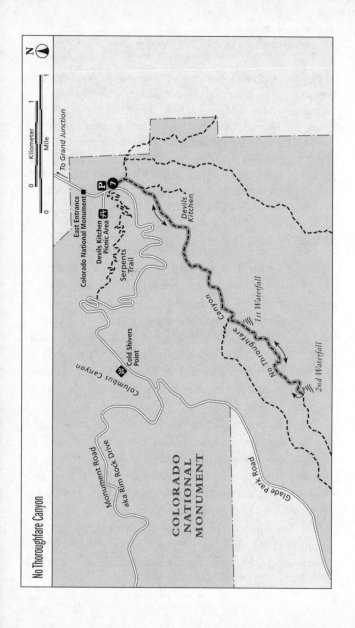

No Thoroughfare Canyon

a tremendous spill that's left beautiful streaks of patina on the sandstone walls. Hundred-year-old Fremont cottonwood trees provide shade during the spring, summer, and fall.

Only experienced hikers should continue on this trail from this point. However, if you're strong enough—and brave enough—to continue upstream, follow the directional arrows to a primitive trail to your right (northwest). Here you'll find the first of many rock cairns (piles of rock marking the trail) that lead to the top of a large, steep outcrop. Watch where you put your hands! There are plenty of prickly pear and barrel cactuses in the rocky crevices.

Once you've reached the top of this outcrop, the trail winds back to the creek bottom. The canyon will broaden and split in another 0.4 mile. Continue along the trail into the canyon to the right, or northwest, and travel 0.6 mile to the second waterfall. There are actually two spills from this fall. If you happen to catch it when it's wet, it can be spectacular. Flash floods, however, are very dangerous in this canyon, so watch the sky!

No Thoroughfare Canyon Trail continues from this point for another 5.5 miles to the upper trailhead at 6,820 feet in elevation. Map-reading skills and backcountry path-finding skills are required from this point, which is beyond the scope of this "best easy day hikes" book.

Miles and Directions

0.0 Start from trailhead at south end of parking area.

0.2 Trail forks; take right fork and follow signs.

0.3 Trail splits again; take right fork, following the directional sign, and continue into No Thoroughfare Canyon.

0.4 Trail drops into creek bed, then crosses from side to side.

1.1 First pool—a slight pour-off in the creek bottom; take the eighty steps up to the right, around the pool to northwest, then back down to the creek bed.

2.0 First waterfall. (***Note:*** If you decide to proceed from here, find the primitive trail to the right, northwest, and follow rock cairns to the top of this steep section and around the waterfall. Drop back to the creek bed and continue upstream for 1 mile to second waterfall. This section requires some path-finding skills.)

2.4 Canyon widens and splits. Stay in the right channel and continue upstream.

3.0 Second waterfall. This is actually a split waterfall, with a pool at the upper waterfall providing the spill for the second fall in front of you.

6.0 Arrive back at trailhead.

8 Serpents Trail

Once dubbed the "Crookedest Road in the World," this trail is now on the National Register of Historic Structures. John Otto was the man responsible for creating the Colorado National Monument in 1911. As its founding father, he single-handedly built many of its trails, including this one.

Distance: 3.7 miles out and back

Hiking time: About 90 minutes up, 45 minutes down

Difficulty: Moderate

Trail surface: Relatively smooth, wide, two-lane dirt and rock road

Best season: Year-round

Other trail users: Foot traffic only

Canine compatibility: No dogs allowed

Fees and permits: 7-day permits for hikers/bikers or cars; yearly monument pass or national parks pass also usable

Maps: USGS Colorado National Monument; Trails Illustrated Colorado National Monument/McInnis Canyons NCA

Trail contacts: Colorado National Monument, Fruita, CO 81521; (970) 858-3616, nps.gov/colm

Finding the trailhead: This trailhead is located just inside the east entrance of the Colorado National Monument on Monument Road (turn left off Broadway after it crosses the Colorado River and proceed 3.3 miles). From the entrance gate, travel 0.2 mile. Park on the left. (*Note:* This is also the parking area for Old Gordon Trail, No Thoroughfare Canyon, Devils Kitchen, and Echo Canyon. Cross the road to find Serpents Trail. If this parking area is full, park across the road in the Devils Kitchen picnic area.) GPS: N39 01.9188' / W108 37.8613'

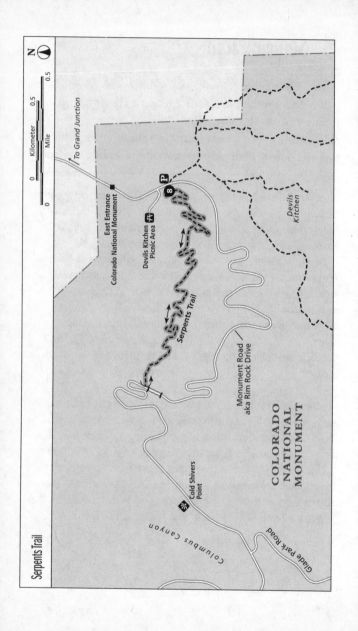

Serpents Trail

N

0   0.5   Kilometer
0   0.5   Mile

To Grand Junction

East Entrance
Colorado National Monument

Devils Kitchen Picnic Area

P

8

Devils
Kitchen

Serpents Trail

Monument Road
aka Rim Rock Drive

Cold Shivers Point

Columbus Canyon

Glade Park Road

COLORADO
NATIONAL
MONUMENT

The Hike

Serpents Trail was used as the main road onto Glade Park and Pinyon Mesa until 1950. It features more than twenty switchbacks cut through the colorful Wingate Sandstone and climbs steadily from east to west. (The total ascent is 794 feet.) It is a strenuous hike on the way up, certainly. It's a cakewalk on the way down, unless you have bad knees.

Views overlooking the Grand Valley from this trail are great, but watch your step and your children at overlooks and steep drop-offs. Occasionally, a hiker will stumble across coyote or bobcat prints in the mud. Don't be surprised to see desert bighorn sheep here, and look up and listen for the fastest bird in the world, the peregrine falcon, which nests and hunts in the canyons of the Colorado National Monument.

Bicycles and motorized vehicles are not allowed on this trail, leaving it to foot-powered pedestrians only. That makes it nice for hikers and runners alike. No one ever gets in anyone else's way on this trail. It's wide and smooth.

Generally, it's just too darn hot to hike this trail in the middle of the day in the middle of summer. Better to hit it early or late in the day at that time of year. The rest of the year, however, it's great any hour.

Miles and Directions

0.0 Start from trailhead across the road from the parking area.

0.1 Start first switchback; plenty more to follow.

1.0 A rock wall constructed by the Civilian Conservation Corp in the 1930s provides a handy rest stop. You are past the halfway mark!

1.8 Reach top of trail; retrace your steps back to the parking area.

9 Liberty Cap/Corkscrew Loop

This is certainly one of the best hikes in the Grand Valley. Is it one of the easiest? Well, it's easy to get to, and if you're in good shape and like to climb, it's an easy hike. With a thousand feet of vertical gain within 1.5 miles, however, this one may stretch the limits of the term "easy."

Distance: 4.4-mile lollipop with tail

Hiking time: About 2 to 3 hours

Difficulty: Moderate to difficult

Trail surface: Wide, hard-packed dirt trail, turning into narrow rock/dirt path

Best season: Year-round, although very hot in the middle of a summer day

Other trail users: Foot traffic only

Canine compatibility: No dogs allowed

Fees and permits: None at this trailhead

Maps: USGS Colorado National Monument; Trails Illustrated Colorado National Monument/McInnis Canyons NCA

Trail contacts: Colorado National Monument, Fruita, CO 81521; (970) 858-3616, nps.gov/colm

Other: If the parking area is full, please choose another hike. This trailhead is located in a quiet, private neighborhood. The residents get upset when people park on the road in front of their homes.

Finding the trailhead: Take Broadway (CO 340) to Redlands Parkway and turn left on South Broadway (or take the Redlands Parkway—24 Road—and it turns into South Broadway). Proceed to Wildwood Drive. Turn left, then veer to the right through a private residential area. The parking area will be on your right. GPS N39 04.0805' / W108 39.6151'

The Hike

A favorite of the locals, Liberty Cap Trail is fun and challenging as it scales the face of the Colorado National Monument on the eastern edge of the Colorado Plateau. It is 1.5 miles from the trailhead to Liberty Cap, a remnant sand dune more than 160 million years old that is slowly succumbing to the forces of erosion. Hikers can continue from Liberty Cap all the way to the top of the Colorado National Monument and the Upper Liberty Cap Trailhead, another six miles up. Most, however, turn around here.

Instead of marching straight back to the vehicle, however, take Corkscrew Trail, the loop on this lollipop hike, for something a little different.

The Corkscrew Trail was built in 1909 by John Otto, the first full-time caretaker of the monument. For decades, this trail provided the only official route through Ute Canyon. Over time, however, the original access to Corkscrew Trail was lost.

In 2005, portions of Corkscrew Trail were rehabilitated by the Volunteers for Outdoor Colorado. Since then, it's gotten quite a bit more use—and a lot more TLC from park service trails crews.

The hike begins from the trailhead on Wildwood Drive and begins to climb almost immediately. In 0.6 mile, the trail climbs behind a giant slab of Kayenta sandstone that has been propped up on its side for tens of thousands of years. Kayenta is the cap rock found through much of this region. Its hard crust protects the softer Wingate sandstone beneath—but not here where it's been propped up on its side.

Zig-zag up the switchbacks for 0.4 mile until you reach the trail crossing with Ute Canyon Trail/Corkscrew Trail.

Here, continue to the right. In another half mile or so, you'll reach Liberty Cap.

On the way back down, you'll return to this same spot. This time, instead of heading back downhill on the Liberty Cap Trail, follow the directional signs and take the Ute Trail/Corkscrew Trail to the right (south) for 0.2 mile. Here, the trails split. Ute Canyon Trail continues to the south and then turns west. Corkscrew Trail goes left and east. Shortly, you'll see why Otto named this the Corkscrew Trail, as it winds its way back down through the hard Precambrian bedrock found here.

Soon, you'll hike through the Precambrian rock and back to sandstone. Follow the signs to where the trail meets up once again with Liberty Cap Trail, and take that back to your vehicle.

Miles and Directions

0.0 Start from west end of parking area at an elevation of 4,815 feet.

0.3 Trail begins to climb steadily.

0.5 Trail levels off for a short way at around 4,930 feet.

0.5 Trail splits with lower Corkscrew Trail; go right (southwest).

0.6 Begin the serious climb with stone steps rising from the bottom of the wash.

1.0 Trail junction with upper Corkscrew/Ute Trails; Go right (west).

1.3 Hike up the sandstone ledge and continue on the switchbacks. Trail levels shortly beyond this ledge.

1.7 Arrive at Liberty Cap, elevation 5,834 feet.

2.4 Back at Liberty Cap/Ute Trail/Corkscrew Trail crossing; this time go right or southeast.

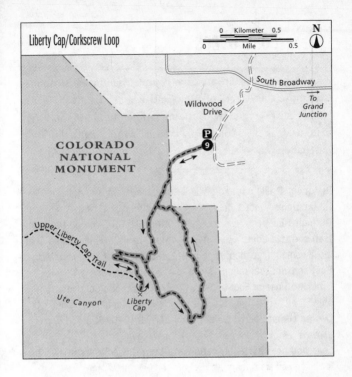

2.6 Trail splits again. To the right is Ute Canyon. Go left (east) and follow Corkscrew Trail.

3.1 A brown carsonite post points the way along the trail.

3.3 Two more brown signposts provide directions.

3.9 Back on the main trail; head right (northeast) and back to parking area.

4.4 Arrive back at parking lot/trailhead.

10 Coke Ovens

The Coke Ovens are massive rounded sandstone structures that show the effects of wind and water over time. If you want a bird's-eye view of the incredible monoliths and rock structures of the Colorado National Monument, this short hike takes you to the very top of the Ovens.

Distance: 1 mile out and back
Hiking time: About 1 hour
Difficulty: Easy
Trail surface: Some stone steps, mostly smooth, gentle dirt path
Best season: Year-round
Other trail users: Foot traffic only
Canine compatibility: No dogs allowed
Fees and permits: 7-day permits for hikers/bikers or cars; yearly monument pass or national parks pass also usable
Maps: USGS Colorado National Monument; Trails Illustrated Colorado National Monument/McInnis Canyons NCA
Trail contacts: Colorado National Monument, Fruita, CO 81521; (970) 858-3616, nps .gov/colm
Other: Guided walks in all seasons except winter

Finding the trailhead: *From Fruita:* Take CO 340 over the Colorado River and into the west entrance of the Colorado National Monument. Proceed to the top of the monument on Rim Rock Drive (Monument Road) and the visitor center. Travel 3.8 miles past the visitor center to the pullout and trailhead on the left. It is also the trailhead for Monument Canyon Trail. *From Grand Junction:* Take Monument Road to the east entrance of the Colorado National Monument. Proceed 15 miles to the trailhead on the right. GPS: N39 04.6629' / W108 43.6891'

The Hike

A short half-mile hike allows you to stand on top of the Coke Ovens, so named because their conical shapes are reminiscent of early twentieth-century ovens used to convert coal into coke, the latter used as an industrial fuel. These rock monoliths of Wingate sandstone clearly show the effects of time and weather when not protected by the cap rock of the Kayenta Formation. Kayenta sandstone is very tightly cemented and much harder than Wingate.

The Coke Ovens Trail shares a trailhead with Upper Monument Canyon Trail. After descending several rock steps into the head of Monument Canyon, the trail splits at 0.2 mile. Upper Monument Canyon Trail traverses to the left, and the Coke Ovens Trail leads to the right, gently paralleling the hillside.

In a few hundred feet, an opening on your left provides great views of Monument Canyon and the Grand Valley beyond. Monument Canyon Trail can also be seen on the opposite wall of the canyon, winding toward the creek bottom, 500 feet below. Keep children and foolish photographers away from this exposed ledge. Continue for another quarter mile to the trail's terminus on top of the closest "oven." Here, a sturdy guard rail prevents further exploration on slippery terrain.

Miles and Directions

0.0 Start from trailhead shared with Upper Monument Canyon Trail.

0.2 Trail splits; go right.

0.5 Trail ends at guard rail. From here retrace steps.

1.0 Arrive back at trailhead.

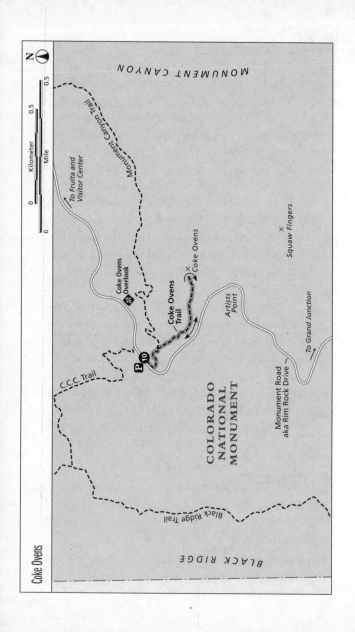

Coke Ovens

N

Kilometer

Mile

0   0.5

To Fruita and
Visitor Center

MONUMENT CANYON

Monument Canyon Trail

Coke Ovens Overlook

C.C.C. Trail

Coke Ovens Trail

Coke Ovens ×

P 10

Artists Point

Squaw Fingers ×

COLORADO
NATIONAL
MONUMENT

Monument Road
aka Rim Rock Drive

To Grand Junction

Black Ridge Trail

BLACK RIDGE

11 Monument Canyon

As the premier hike in the Colorado National Monument, Monument Canyon takes hikers beneath many of the park's major rock sculptures, where Independence Monument, Kissing Couple, and the Coke Ovens tower overhead. It's best to leave a vehicle at each end of this hike, and shuttle one vehicle back after the 6-mile trek downhill.

Distance: 6 miles one way

Hiking time: About 2.5 to 4 hours

Difficulty: Easy to moderate

Trail surface: Relatively smooth rock and dirt backcountry trail

Best season: Year-round, although very hot in the middle of a summer day

Other trail users: Foot traffic only

Canine compatibility: No dogs allowed

Fees and permits: 7-day permits for hikers/bikers or cars; yearly monument pass or national parks pass also usable

Maps: USGS Colorado National Monument; Trails Illustrated Colorado National Monument/McInnis Canyons NCA

Trail contacts: Colorado National Monument, Fruita, CO 81521; (970) 858-3616, nps .gov/colm

Other: Guided walks all seasons except winter

Finding the trailhead: Upper Trailhead: *From Grand Junction:* Travel through the east entrance of the Colorado National Monument on Monument Road. The upper trailhead is on the right-hand side of the road, 15 miles from the east entrance. *From Fruita:* Take CO 340 to the west entrance of the monument and travel 3.8 miles past the visitor center to the trailhead on the left. This is also the trailhead for the Coke Ovens Trail. GPS: N39 04.6602' /W108 43.6873'

Lower Trailhead: *From Grand Junction:* Take Grand Avenue over the Colorado River Bridge, where it becomes CO 340 (Broadway). Stay on this until you reach the Monument Canyon Trailhead turn, approximately 7.5 miles. The turn is located just past (northwest of) the Deer Park subdivision on the left. (It appears as if you're turning into someone's private driveway, but follow the signs and continue 0.1 mile to trailhead parking.) *From Fruita:* Take CO 340 past the west entrance of the monument and proceed 2.1 miles, then turn right just beyond mile marker 5 onto a dirt road that appears to be a driveway. Continue 0.1 mile to the parking area and trailhead. GPS: N39 06.5231′/W108 42.0876′

The Hike

A one-way hike of six miles from the top of Monument Canyon to its mouth in the valley below allows hikers to descend through a sequence of sedimentary rock layers that span 50 million years—from the Upper Jurassic to the Upper Triassic Periods of the Mesozoic Era.

This easy hiking trail descends 1,440 feet, from 6,140 feet above sea level to 4,700 feet. Much of the descent comes within the first mile as hikers view the Coke Ovens across the canyon to the south. After that, the route follows a gentle course and in very short order makes a sweeping left turn, heading north around the base of a sheer cliff to reveal a number of tall, freestanding monoliths. The first is Kissing Couple—two sandstone towers that appear entwined in a lover's embrace. Next to this is Praying Hands.

Further into the canyon, hikers encounter the iconic and impressive Independence Monument. This structure was once part of a massive rock wall that separated Monument and Wedding Canyons. Slowly, as the forces of erosion enlarged these canyons millions of years ago, the dividing wall was narrowed and weakened. Eventually, the wall was breached and parts of it collapsed. Independence Monument survived as a freestanding monolith.

For the next 2 miles, the trail descends on the right (south) side of the Island, what's left of that wall between Monument and Wedding Canyons. This large and colorful canyon wall is actually a monocline (downward slopping rock layers). Soon, hikers will travel through the harder and darker 1.7-billion-year-old Precambrian rock that lies beneath the reddish Chinle Formation. This is the base rock here and among the oldest rocks on the Colorado Plateau.

In 5 miles, hikers reach the mouth of the canyon, filled with 150-year-old Fremont cottonwoods. The trail here takes a sharp left turn and follows a very tall fence along the west side of the Deer Park subdivision and back to the lower trailhead and parking area. This is a great area to watch for desert bighorn sheep, which are found in this area year-round.

Miles and Directions

0.0 Start at trailhead at southwest end of parking area.

0.2 Go left (to the right is Coke Ovens Trail).

0.2 Sign in for this backcountry trail.

0.6 Cross creek bed at an elevation of 5,521 feet.

3.4 Reach the base of Independence Monument (elevation 5,281 feet); go right to continue on Monument Canyon Trail.

5.0 Arrive at mouth of canyon beneath 150-year-old Fremont cottonwoods; go left and follow tall fence line adjacent to subdivision.

5.4 Wedding Canyon Trail leads to the left; go right to Monument Canyon Trailhead parking.

6.0 Arrive at lower Monument Canyon Trailhead.

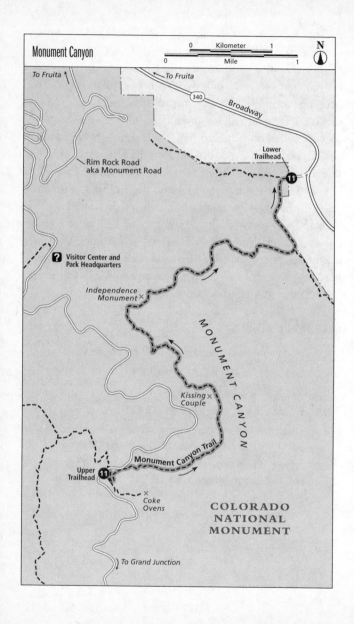

Monument Canyon

0   Kilometer   1

0   Mile   1

N

To Fruita

To Fruita

340 Broadway

Rim Rock Road
aka Monument Road

Lower
Trailhead

11

? Visitor Center and
Park Headquarters

Independence
Monument ×

MONUMENT CANYON

Kissing ×
Couple

Upper
Trailhead

11

Monument Canyon Trail

× Coke
Ovens

COLORADO
NATIONAL
MONUMENT

To Grand Junction

Adjacent to Colorado National Monument in Grand Junction and Fruita

12 Riggs Hill

Elmer Riggs and his crew of paleontologists from the Field Museum in Chicago discovered and excavated huge fossilized bones of a previously unknown dinosaur, *Brachiosaurus altithorax,* on this hill in 1900. Still on display outside the Field Museum in Chicago, the 75-foot-long plant-eater weighed 44 tons. A self-guided tour of Riggs Hill leads to sites where these bones, as well as partial skeletons of *Stegosaurus* and *Allosaurus,* were found.

Distance: 1.1-mile loop

Hiking time: About 30 to 45 minutes

Difficulty: Easy to moderate

Trail surface: Hard packed dirt trail, turning into narrow rock/dirt path; some loose gravel

Best season: Year-round, although very hot in the middle of a summer day

Other trail users: Foot traffic only

Canine compatibility: Dogs allowed on leash; owners to pick up after pets

Fees and permits: None

Maps: USGS Colorado National Monument, Latitude 40° Fruita/Grand Junction

Trail contacts: Museum of Western Colorado, 462 Ute Ave., Grand Junction, CO, 81501; (970) 242-0971, museumofwesternco.com

Finding the trailhead: Take Broadway (CO 340) to the Redlands Parkway and turn left on South Broadway (or take the Redlands Parkway (24 Road) and stay on it since it turns into South Broadway). Proceed 0.2 mile past South Camp Road. Trailhead parking is on the right. GPS: N39 04.3784' / W108 38.9599'

The Hike

Dinosaurs thrived here 150 million years ago on a warm and humid floodplain. Over time, seas, lakes, and rivers deposited thousands of feet of sediment, and entire mountain ranges eroded. Remnants of these great dinosaurs turned to rock, their bones fossilized.

Riggs found a bone bonanza here in 1900 when he and his party found the huge fossilized bones of a previously unknown dinosaur, *Brachiosaurus altithorax*. By 1937, remains of a *Stegosaurus* and *Allosaurus* were also found here.

This trail traces time as a self-guided tour discusses the geologic history of the area. It begins to the left of the blank kiosk on the southwest edge of the parking area. Inside a sign-in box, hikers will (with luck) find a brochure and the *Riggs Hill Trail Map* provided by the Museum of Western Colorado.

The single-track dirt trail travels inside the fence along South Broadway. Within the first 0.2 mile, visitors will be led past four stops on the eight-point self-guided tour. The fourth spot is the site of the *Brachiosaurus altithorax* discovery. It is marked with a plaque dedicated to Riggs and a life-size plaster replica of the *Brachiosaurus* backbone he found here.

The trail continues along South Broadway for a short way before rounding the western edge of the hill to the right and climbing to the next two viewing spots. Within a half mile, visitors reach a ridge and shade shelter between the twin hilltops of Riggs Hill. To the right, hikers can climb the short embankment to the top of the hill, which provides a 360-degree view that includes the Colorado National Monument, Book Cliffs, Grand Mesa, and Grand Valley stretched out below.

Hikers then return to the shade shelter and scramble down the loose rock and gravel trail to the parking area, or continue up a single-track dirt trail toward the top of the next hilltop to the east. In a quarter mile up the second hill, a well-used trail turns hard right and continues downhill toward the parking area. Be careful as there's plenty of loose rock and dirt on this stretch, as well.

Numerous social trails cross this area. The route described here is the most well used.

Miles and Directions

0.0 Start next to blank kiosk at southwest end of parking area at an elevation of 4,694 feet.

0.2 Trail leads to the left, parallel to South Broadway and reaches the fourth marker on the eight-marker trek here, the site of Riggs's *Brachiosaurus altithorax* discovery.

0.3 Go right after rounding the bottom of the hill and hike uphill to next marker.

0.4 Climb 50 feet to marker 6. Watch out for loose rock left after flash flood.

0.5 Trail junction on the saddle between two high points at 4,814 feet. To the left is the main trail and shade shelter. A short spur to the right leads to the top of the hill at 4,918 feet.

0.8 Hike back to shade shelter. At this point, hikers can scramble down the embankment back to the parking lot, to end the shorter hike at 0.9 mile or hike up the sandstone ledge on the single-track trail leading northeast.

0.9 Turn right and drop back down toward the parking area. Be careful of loose rock in this area.

1.1 Arrive back at trailhead.

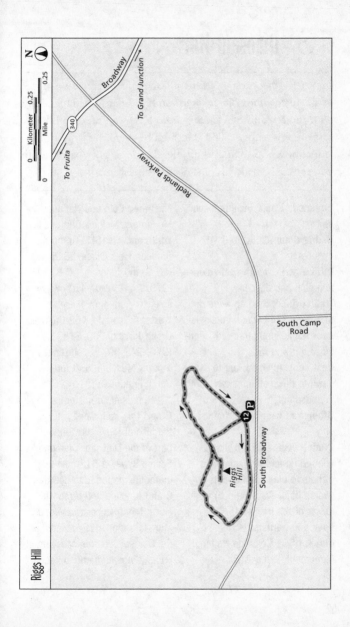

Riggs Hill

To Grand Junction

Broadway

340

To Fruita

Redlands Parkway

South Camp Road

12 P

South Broadway

Riggs Hill

N

Kilometer   0.25
0

Mile   0.25
0

13 Dinosaur Hill

In 1901, paleontologist Elmer Riggs uncovered two-thirds of an *Apatosaurus (Brontosaurus)* on Dinosaur Hill. This, along with the remains of a *Brachiosaurus* Riggs found on a hill just east of here—now called Riggs Hill—were the largest dinosaurs known to man at the time. This trail goes past the site where Riggs made his *Apatosaurus* discovery.

Distance: 1 mile, including spur trail

Hiking time: About 30 to 45 minutes

Difficulty: Easy with some elevation gain and descent

Trail surface: Smooth, wide dirt path for a short way, then single-track backcountry trail with some loose dirt and rock

Best season: Open year-round, dawn to dusk, although very hot in midsummer

Other trail users: Foot traffic only

Canine compatibility: Dogs allowed under leash control; owners to pick up after pets (waste bags available near vault toilets at the trailhead)

Fees and permits: None

Maps: USGS Colorado National Monument, Fruita; Trails Illustrated Colorado National Monument/McInnis Canyons NCA

Trail contacts: BLM Grand Junction Field Office, 2815 H Rd., Grand Junction, CO 81506; (970) 244-3000, blm.gov/co/st/en/fo/gjfo.html. Museum of Western Colorado, 462 Ute Ave., Grand Junction, CO, 81501; (970) 242-0971. Also Dinosaur Journey Museum, 550 Jurassic Court, Fruita CO; (970) 858-7282, museumofwesternco.com.

Other: This trail, along with the hike at Riggs Hill, forms part of the Dinosaur Diamond Scenic Byway, a 512-mile-long diamond-shaped loop between Grand Junction and three Utah cities: Moab, Price, and Vernal. More information is available at the Dinosaur Journey Museum in Fruita, dinosaurdiamond.net.

Finding the trailhead: From Fruita, take CO 340 south across the Colorado River for 0.5 mile. Turn left onto Dinosaur Hill Turnoff, across the highway and 0.2 mile past Kings View Estates and Kodels Canyon Trailhead. GPS: N39 07.9900' / W108 44.1821'

The Hike

In 1891, a local Grand Junction newspaper documented the discovery of "agatized bones of the mastadon [*sic*]" in a nearby cave along with eight mummified bodies of the genus Homo, 11 feet tall. In fact, these were all dinosaur bones, but such local legends had spread for years until 1900, when the first scientific work was conducted in Mesa County: Paleontologist Elmer Riggs collected a forelimb and shoulder blade of *Camarasaurus* near what would soon become the Colorado National Monument. He then uncovered the first *Brachiosaurus* at Riggs Hill on the Redlands in Grand Junction. Returning in 1901, he uncovered two-thirds of an *Apatosaurus (Brontosaurus)* here at Dinosaur Hill.

Apatosaurus means "deceptive lizard." It was an 85-foot-long quadruped with a long neck and long whip-like tail.

This loop trail leads to a number of informational signs and begins behind the kiosk at the southwest side of the parking area, at an elevation of 4,578 feet. At the first intersection, turn right and travel up the hill 0.2 mile to the first shade shelter. A second shade shelter is found at 0.3 mile at 4,709 feet. Most of the climbing is now done. At 0.6 mile, visitors can view the excavation site where Riggs found the *Apatosaurus* bones. The trail then leads back to the parking area. To complete a full mile-long hike, trek back up the start of the trail and turn left at the first intersection, taking this spur trail to its terminus at the west and north end of Dinosaur Hill. This leads to a spot where more dinosaur bones were once

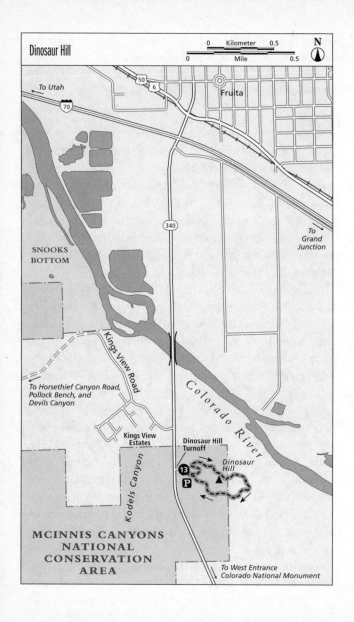

Dinosaur Hill

0 — Kilometer — 0.5
0 — Mile — 0.5

N

To Utah

50 6

Fruita

70

To Grand Junction

SNOOKS BOTTOM

340

Kings View Road

To Horsethief Canyon Road, Pollock Bench, and Devils Canyon

Colorado River

Kings View Estates

Kodels Canyon

Dinosaur Hill Turnoff

Dinosaur Hill

13

P

MCINNIS CANYONS NATIONAL CONSERVATION AREA

To West Entrance Colorado National Monument

discovered, then vandalized and stolen, probably by 1960. Return to the parking area to complete this trip.

Miles and Directions

0.0 Begin trail at kiosk at southwest end of parking area, next to vault toilets. Turn right at first intersection and head uphill toward informational signs.

0.2 Reach first shade shelter.

0.3 Arrive at second shade shelter at 4,709 feet.

0.6 View excavated bones from 70-foot-long *Apatosaurus*.

0.8 Arrive back at parking area and informational kiosk, then travel back on beginning of trail, taking the first left to a spur trail leading to a vandalized discovery site. Retrace steps.

1.0 Arrive back at parking area.

McInnis Canyons National Conservation Area (front country northwest of GJ)

14 Kodels Canyon

Kodels Canyon Trail actually begins in the BLM's McInnis Canyons National Conservation Area and travels into the Colorado National Monument near its west entrance.

Distance: 4 miles out and back
Hiking time: About 2 to 3 hours
Difficulty: Easy to start, strenuous and difficult once you enter the national monument
Trail surface: Narrow dirt backcountry path
Best season: Year-round
Other trail users: Horseback riders, mountain bikers up to national monument boundary; hikers only beyond that point
Canine compatibility: Dogs allowed under control in NCA, but not in national monument.
Fees and permits: None

Maps: USGS Colorado National Monument; Trails Illustrated Colorado National Monument/McInnis Canyons NCA
Trail contacts: BLM Grand Junction Field Office, 2815 H Rd., Grand Junction, CO 81506; (970) 244-3000, blm.gov/co/st/en/fo/gjfo.html. Colorado National Monument, Fruita, CO 81521; (970) 858-3616, nps.gov/colm.
Special considerations: Some backcountry pathfinding skills may be required toward the end of this hike.

Finding the trailhead: The parking area for the Kodels Canyon Trailhead is really just the barrow ditch adjacent to CO 340 next to the Kings View Estates subdivision in Fruita, 0.4 mile south of the Colorado River. GPS: N 39 13.5210' / W108 73.8661'

The Hike

A one-mile hike from the parking area will take you into a desert wilderness with very few people, loads of wildflowers, and a plethora of towering rock walls, spires, and windows that frame the fascinating canyonlands of the upper Colorado River Plateau.

At the trailhead, you'll spy a Bureau of Land Management sign directing you onto a trail system established for Kodels, Devils, Flume, and Pollock Bench Trails. The Kodels Canyon Trail within the BLM's McInnis National Conservation Area ranges in elevation from 4,500 feet to about 5,100 feet. This trail, however, continues into the Colorado National Monument's westernmost canyon—Kodels—just west of the west entrance to the national monument.

The first part of the trail is easy, but the last section is much more strenuous and will require some backcountry pathfinding skills. At the start of the trail, head west, then south and down toward the wash. The trail forks in several places, and BLM signs mark trails K1 and K2 at the first fork. Take the K1 stretch until you reach K7. (The "K" stands for Kodels, just as "D" designates trails in Devils Canyon and "P" stands for Pollock Canyon trails.)

As you continue on K7, you eventually come to the Colorado National Monument boundary.

When you cross a wooden BLM fence under a power line, travel toward the left (east) into the mouth of Kodels Canyon. From here, turn right and hike directly up the canyon until you come to a second fence, this one of old barbed wire.

At this second fence, hike through the gate and into the canyon. You'll climb up, into, and over the tremendous "basement rocks" of this formation, as well as the dark-colored Precambrian granites that are around 1.7 billion years old.

You can hike around this steep, difficult section by taking the right-leaning path that will lead you beneath an impressive stone monolith and deeper into the canyon.

In front of you and to your right, you'll see a massive rock spire. Beyond that, the canyon splits into two major circular box ends. Pick your way to the right-hand canyon end. You'll have to scramble up another 250 feet in about a half mile to enter a tremendous alcove hidden behind very large cottonwoods at the end of this canyon.

Miles and Directions

0.0 Begin at parking area, travel 80 yards up the hill, then turn south.

0.2 Take right fork and follow trail labeled K1.

0.5 Cross the bottom of the gully and continue forward, to the southwest.

0.6 Turn left on trail marked K7/K1 (K4 continues to the west).

1.0 Colorado National Monument boundary; cross through fence and stay left.

1.4 Reach second fence line. To the right is an old gate leading into the national monument.

1.5 Trail leads to the right of a steep section of dark-colored Precambrian granite.

2.1 Canyon splits; go right. No formal trail here. Bushwack to the top of the alcove.

2.4 Arrive at alcove. Retrace steps.

4.0 Arrive back at parking area.

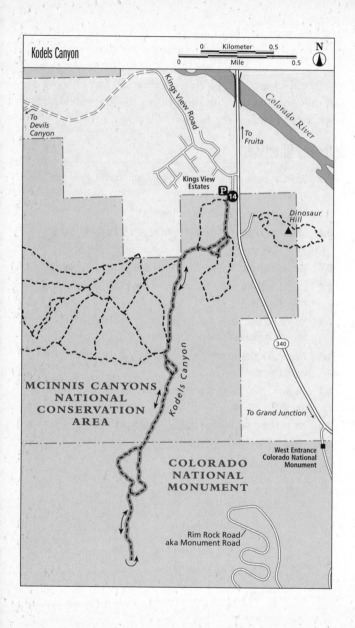

Kodels Canyon

0   Kilometer   0.5
0   Mile   0.5

N

To Devils Canyon

Kings View Road

Colorado River

To Fruita

Kings View Estates

P 14

Dinosaur Hill

340

Kodels Canyon

MCINNIS CANYONS
NATIONAL
CONSERVATION
AREA

To Grand Junction

COLORADO
NATIONAL
MONUMENT

West Entrance
Colorado National
Monument

Rim Rock Road /
aka Monument Road

15 Devils Canyon

Located in the front country of the BLM's 123,000-acre McInnis Canyons National Conservation Area, Devils Canyon is one of four great canyons—along with Kodels, Flume Creek, and Pollock—that are easily accessible from the same road. Trails here vary in length and difficulty, to the delight of hikers young and old.

Distance: 2.5-mile lollipop
Hiking time: About 1 hour
Difficulty: Easy
Trail surface: Wide, hard-packed gravel; loose sand part of the way
Best season: Year-round, although very hot in midsummer
Other trail users: Foot and horseback traffic only; use limited to designated trails in this area
Canine compatibility: Dogs allowed under control and on leash around others and during spring (lambing season for desert bighorn sheep); owners to pick up after their pets
Fees and permits: None
Maps: USGS Colorado National Monument, Fruita, Ruby Canyon, and Battleship Rock; Trails Illustrated Colorado National Monument/McInnis Canyons NCA; BLM *Devils, Flume, and Pollock Bench Trail System* (brochure)
Trail contacts: BLM Grand Junction Field Office, 2815 H Rd., Grand Junction, CO 81506; (970) 244-3000, blm.gov/co/st/en/fo/gjfo.html
Special considerations: Pack insect repellant as biting gnats can be nasty from May through August. Temperatures can exceed 100 degrees Fahrenheit during the summer. And remember, you may be lathered in sunscreen and wearing a wide-brimmed hat, sunglasses, T-shirt, and shorts, but your dog is wearing a fur coat!

Finding the trailhead: From Grand Junction, take I-70 west to Fruita (exit 19) and travel south on CO 340 over the Colorado River to Kings View Estates (1.3 miles). Turn right on Kings View Road. Go through the subdivision, and when the pavement ends, the road veers to the left past the Fruita Open Space Park and becomes Horsethief Canyon Road. Travel 0.6 mile to the Devils Canyon turn and parking area. GPS: N39 08.3934' /W108 45.4168'

The Hike

While there are hundreds of miles of hiking trails in this area, the route here is a 2.5-mile lollipop loop that's gentle on the knees and a scenic trip the entire family can enjoy. Parts of this trail are hard-packed and wheelchair accessible.

The hike begins at the western end of the parking area. Travel 0.2 mile to a BLM kiosk, which discusses the importance of sharing this country with a variety of wildlife, including desert bighorn sheep, collared lizards, and golden eagles.

In another tenth of a mile, hikers will encounter the first of many trail markers. (*Note:* All trails labeled with the letter "D" are for Devils Canyon, "P" trails go to Pollock Canyon, "F" trails go into Flume Creek Canyon, and "K" trails go to Kodels Canyon.)

At this first marker, take trail D5 to the right. Follow D5 for a short distance to the trail labeled D4 and go left. This trail splits in another 0.4 mile. Continue forward on the right fork. In another 0.2 mile, D4 splits again. This time, go left.

In 0.6 mile, D4 crosses D1. Take D1 to the left for 0.4 mile. At this point, hikers will come to an intersection with trails labeled D2, D3, and K1. Continue forward on D1 and follow this back to the parking area.

This short, easy trail bounces in and out of the mouth of Devils Canyon, and as the light changes throughout the day, so do the colors and shades of red, rust, brown, and tan.

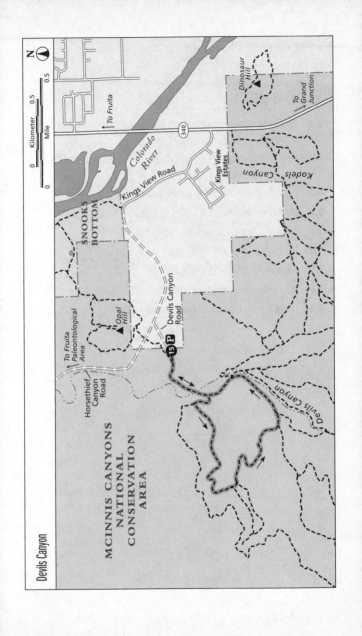

Devils Canyon

MCINNIS CANYONS NATIONAL CONSERVATION AREA

Horsethief Canyon Road

To Fruita Paleontological Area

Opal Hill

Devils Canyon Road

15 P

Devils Canyon

SNOOKS BOTTOM

Colorado River

Kings View Road

Kings View Estates

Kodels Canyon

340

To Fruita

Dinosaur Hill

To Grand Junction

N

0   0.5   Kilometer
0   0.5   Mile

This area is especially stunning at sunup and sundown. Don't forget your camera!

Miles and Directions

0.0 Start from trailhead at west end of parking area (4,536 feet in elevation) following trail D1.

0.2 Reach BLM kiosk stressing importance of sharing this country with wildlife.

0.3 Go right on trail labeled D5 at intersection of D1 and D5.

0.5 Go left on trail labeled D4 at intersection of D5 and D4.

0.8 D4 splits; continue forward (right fork).

1.0 Go left again as D4 splits once more.

1.6 D4 crosses D1. Take D1 to the left.

2.0 D1 intersects with D2, D3, and K1. Continue forward on D1.

2.5 Arrive back at Devils Canyon parking area.

16 Fruita Paleontological Area

A loop trail slightly longer than a half mile can offer up a lot of learning. Meandering through the Fruita Paleontological Area, this trail features twenty interpretive signs describing dinosaurs and other creatures that roamed the area 150 million years ago. This world-class fossil site contains a prolific record of Jurassic microvertebrates.

Distance: 0.7-mile self-guided loop
Hiking time: About 45 minutes
Difficulty: Easy
Trail surface: Rock, sand, and gravel
Best season: Year-round, although very hot in summer
Other trail users: Foot traffic only
Canine compatibility: Dogs allowed under control
Fees and permits: None

Maps: USGS Colorado National Monument; Trails Illustrated Colorado National Monument/McInnis Canyons NCA
Trail contacts: BLM Grand Junction Field Office, 2815 H Rd., Grand Junction, CO 81506; (970) 244-3000, blm.gov/co/st/en/fo/gjfo.html. Also Museum of Western Colorado, 462 Ute Ave., Grand Junction, CO 81501; (970) 242-0971, museumofwesternco.com.

Finding the trailhead: Take CO 340 1.2 miles south of Fruita to Kings View Road. Turn right. In 1.2 miles, Kings View Road turns into Horsethief Canyon Road. Continue on this for another mile. Parking and trailhead will appear on your left. GPS: N39 09.0839' /W108 45.7843'

The Hike

This area preserves a greater diversity of prehistoric life from the Jurassic Period of 150 million years ago than any other

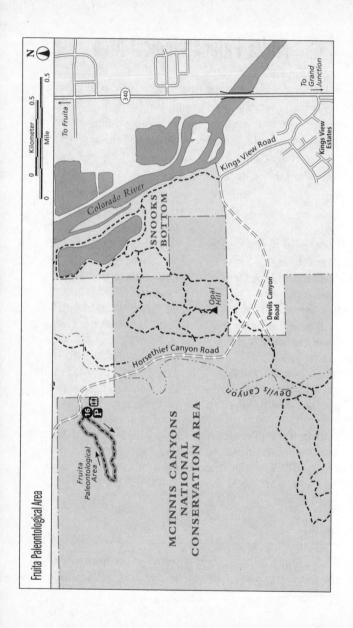

Fruita Paleontological Area

known place on earth. Based on the variety of fossils discovered here, this spot is paleontological nirvana. In fact, one of the most unique fossils ever discovered—the *Fruitafossor windscheffeli*—was unearthed here and named after Grand Junction resident Wally Windscheffel in 1998.

Wally discovered the fossilized remains of an animal about 6 inches (15 cm) long and weighing about 30 grams (about 1 ounce). Slightly longer and slimmer than a hairy-tailed mouse, it was a digger, hiding in burrows from larger dinosaurs. Mammals coexisting with *Fruitafossor* mostly ate insects. Other types of animals living here back then included crocodiles, turtles, lizards, frogs, and flying reptiles, and the earth's first known birds.

One hundred and fifty million years later, this hike is as close as you'll ever get to the once formidable meat-eating *Ceratosaurus maghicornis*, weighing in at 1.5 tons and measuring 17 feet long, or the diminutive (at 8 feet long) plant-eating *Dryosaurus*, or even the *Fruitafossor windscheffeli*.

The route is obvious and easy to follow. Simply hop from one interpretive sign to the next.

Miles and Directions

0.0 Start from parking area and trailhead and proceed from the BLM kiosk in the parking area to the first interpretive sign.

0.3 Trail turns right and heads up hill.

0.5 Follow old, two-lane jeep road.

0.6 Take narrow path back to parking area.

0.7 Arrive back at trailhead.

17   Pollock Bench

The Devils Canyon and Pollock Bench trail system is an intricate network of trails that explore the yawning mouths of both Devils and Pollock Canyons in the front country of the 123,000-acre McInnis Canyons National Conservation Area. Managed by the Bureau of Land Management, this roadless area is shared with horseback riders.

Distance: 6-mile loop

Hiking time: About 2 to 3 hours

Difficulty: Easy

Trail surface: First part of loop on old jeep trail; narrow back-country path on return

Best season: Year-round, although possibly very hot in midsummer, snowy/muddy in winter

Other trail users: Foot traffic and horseback riders only

Canine compatibility: Dogs allowed under control and on leash around others or during spring (lambing season for desert bighorn sheep); owners to pick up after their dogs

Fees and permits: None

Maps: USGS Colorado National Monument, Fruita, Ruby Canyon, and Battleship Rock; Trails Illustrated Colorado National Monument/McInnis Canyons NCA; BLM *Devils, Flume, and Pollock Bench Trail System* (brochure)

Trail contacts: BLM Grand Junction Field Office, 2815 H Rd., Grand Junction, CO 81506; (970) 244-3000, blm.gov/co/st/en/fo/gjfo.html

Special considerations: Pack insect repellant as biting gnats can be nasty from May through August. Temperatures can exceed 100 degrees Fahrenheit. You may be lathered in sunscreen and wearing a wide-brimmed hat, sunglasses, T-shirt, and shorts, but your dog is wearing a fur coat!

Finding the trailhead: Take I-70 west to exit 19, Fruita. Travel south across the river on CO 340 for 1.3 miles to Kings View Estates subdivision. Turn right (west) and travel through the subdivision. When the pavement ends, veer to the left past the City of Fruita Open Space Park, then follow the signs toward Horsethief Canyon State Wildlife Area. The Pollock Bench Trailhead parking lot is located 3.3 miles from the subdivision, just before you approach the main entrance of Horsethief Canyon State Wildlife Area. You'll pass the Devils Canyon Trailhead and the Fruita Paleontological Area along the way. GPS: N39 09.3463' / W108 46.7136'

The Hike

This excellent 6-mile loop leads hikers up an old jeep trail, across slickrock, and through pinyon-juniper covered hillsides between two deep gorges in the landscape—Pollock Canyon and Flume Creek Canyon. This is called the "front country" of the McInnis Canyons National Conservation Area because of its easy access to Fruita and Grand Junction. This trail is also considered easy, yet these canyons are deep, steep, rugged, and wild.

An intricate network of well-marked trails exists here. The "P" trails lead to Pollock Canyon, "F" trails are Flume Creek Canyon trails, "R" trails lead to Rattlesnake Canyon, "D" trails go to Devils Canyon, and "K" trails go to Kodels Canyon.

This route is not as rugged and steep as some. It begins at the northeast end of the parking area and, within a few dozen yards, it splits. Take P1 to the right and up the hillside above the parking lot.

Elevation at the trailhead is 4,469 feet above sea level. Hike up the 7 percent grade hill and acclimate to the altitude. You'll reach 5,265 feet—15 feet short of 1 mile above sea level—at the peak of this trail in 2.7 miles.

At 0.4 mile, cut through the gate and hike about 60 yards. Here, F1 leads to the left. Instead, go right on P1 and hike up the ledge on the far side of this draw. At 0.6 mile, the trail levels off on the rim of the canyon bowl that hikers will circumnavigate in a counterclockwise direction on this trek.

At 1.6 miles, the trail intersects with R1, which leads to a rugged 10-mile trek to Rattlesnake Canyon Arches Trail (for an alternate route to Rattlesnake Canyon, see hike 18). Continue on P1.

At 2.3 miles, hikers come to a ledge with great views looking southwest into the east and west forks of Pollock Canyon. Continue on the trail for another 0.4 mile to the trail intersection with F2. Here, trail P1 drops to the right and lower bench below the previous view point. It's a great trail, but longer and more difficult than F2. Go left on F2, where the trail here becomes a single-track, backcountry dirt trail.

At 3.8 miles, the trail delivers hikers beneath a huge and intricate rock wall before continuing downstream. Just past the 5-mile mark, F1 intersects with P2. Here, hikers can go either way back to the vehicle, 0.9 mile away.

Miles and Directions

0.0 Start from trailhead at southeast end of parking area near BLM kiosk (4,469 feet in elevation). About 30 yards past the trailhead, trails labeled P1 and F1 split. Go right on P1.

0.3 Hike up the 7 percent grade hill and acclimate to the altitude.

0.4 Pass through the gate, and then go right in about 60 paces, continuing on P1.

1.6 Go left at the trail intersection with Pollock Canyon/Rattle-snake Arches, continuing on Pollock Bench loop.

2.3 Reach an elevation of 5,175 feet and enjoy the views looking southwest into the east fork of Pollock Canyon.

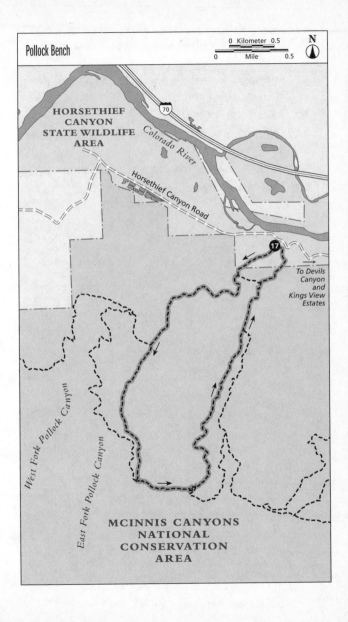

Pollock Bench

0 Kilometer 0.5
0 Mile 0.5

N

HORSETHIEF
CANYON
STATE WILDLIFE
AREA

Colorado River

I-70

Horsethief Canyon Road

17

To Devils
Canyon and
Kings View
Estates

West Fork Pollock Canyon

East Fork Pollock Canyon

MCINNIS CANYONS
NATIONAL
CONSERVATION
AREA

2.7 Arrive at the trail's peak elevation, 5,265 feet. When the trail splits shortly, go left on the single-track trail marked F2 (Flume Creek Canyon).

3.2 Switchbacks will lead you down and back toward the Grand Valley and Colorado River.

3.3 Trail splits; go left on F1.

3.8 Trail travels beneath large freestanding rock wall and continues downstream.

5.1 Trail splits. Hikers can go either way back to the vehicle.

6.0 Arrive back at trailhead.

McInnis Canyons/ Blackridge Wilderness Area (backcountry northwest of GJ)

18 Rattlesnake Canyon Arches Loop

Seven major sandstone arches display their age, majesty, and delicacy on this great hike into the Black Ridge Wilderness Area. The 75,500-acre wilderness forms the core of the 123,000-acre McInnis Canyons National Conservation Area, designated by Congress in 2000 as "a nationally significant resource."

Distance: 6-mile loop
Hiking time: About 3 to 5 hours
Difficulty: Moderate; one short (0.2-mile) rocky and steep section
Trail surface: Old jeep road for the first half mile; rocky, steep 0.2-mile stretch; then easy, sandy, backcountry trail
Best season: Late April until the first snow flies (*Note:* Motorized travel is prohibited from Feb 15 to Apr 15. Rattlesnake Arches Trail can be accessed from the Pollock Bench Trailhead during those months.)
Other trail users: Horseback riders (rarely because of steep drop to the lower bench)
Canine compatibility: Allowed under control
Fees and permits: None
Maps: USGS Mack, Ruby Canyon, and Battleship Rock; Trails Illustrated Colorado National Monument/McInnis Canyons NCA
Trail contacts: BLM Grand Junction Field Office, 2815 H Rd., Grand Junction, CO 81506; (970) 244-3000, blm.gov/co/st/en/nca/mcnca.html
Special considerations: While this area is only 36 miles from downtown Grand Junction and 23 miles from Fruita, the last 2 miles of the 10-mile Black Ridge dirt road is mean, nasty, and impassable when wet. A high-clearance, four-wheel-drive vehicle is required. The drive takes 1 hour, 40 minutes from Grand Junction.

You can reach Rattlesnake Canyon Arches via a 15.5-mile out-and-back hike from the Pollock Bench Trail, but it's not an "easy" hike.

Finding the trailhead: From Grand Junction, take I-70 west to exit 19, Fruita, then turn left onto CO 340 and follow the signs to the Colorado National Monument (south). Travel 2.5 miles to the west entrance and turn right. From the entrance gate, travel on Rim Rock Road 4.1 miles to the visitor center, and then continue another 6.4 miles to the Glade Park Store cutoff and Black Ridge Road turnoff. Turn right and travel a short distance to Black Ridge Road. Turn right again. Stay on this main dirt road for 10.1 miles. The last two miles are very rugged. A high-clearance, four-wheel-drive vehicle is required. GPS: N39 08.2309' / W108 50.0051'

The Hike

Rattlesnake Canyon Arches Trail is adventurous and fascinating. Its colorful geological features include spires, windows, gorgeous giant alcoves, and at least seven fabulous arches (although some literature notes there are actually eleven arches here).

A trip through Rattlesnake Canyon is a kaleidoscopic journey through time and earth—from the upper ends of Black Ridge along the green, gray, and purple Morrison formation, down through rust-colored Entrada sandstone, and beneath the spectacular Wingate formation with its towering stone walls.

Pinyon, juniper, sagebrush, and riparian vegetation in this area provide habitat for mule deer, mountain lion, and a herd of bighorn sheep as well as peregrine falcons and bald and golden eagles.

From the trailhead at the west end of the parking area, the trail follows an old jeep road winding down from the top bench for 0.5 mile to a trail junction. For those not willing to take the 0.2-mile downward plunge to the next bench below, go left to the First Arch overlook, 0.5 mile away. For

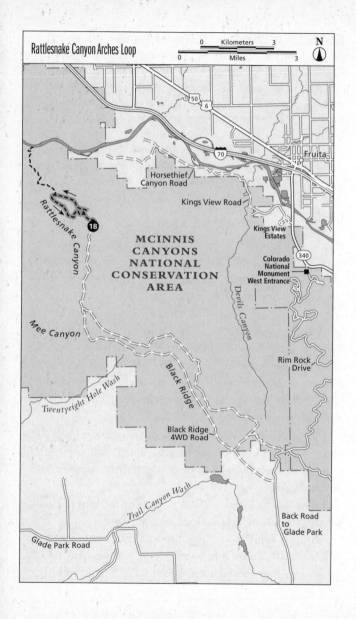

Rattlesnake Canyon Arches Loop

Kilometers
0   3
0   Miles   3

N

50
6
70
Fruita

Horsethief
Canyon Road

Kings View Road

Rattlesnake Canyon

18

Kings View
Estates

340

Colorado
National
Monument
West Entrance

MCINNIS
CANYONS
NATIONAL
CONSERVATION
AREA

Devils Canyon

Rim Rock
Drive

Mee Canyon

Black Ridge

Twentyeight Hole Wash

Black Ridge
4WD Road

Trail Canyon Wash

Back Road
to
Glade Park

Glade Park Road

everyone else, turn right and travel 0.2 mile down a steep, rocky set of switchbacks to the next junction with the Pollock Canyon Trail.

Here, go left and follow a narrow, sandy, backcountry path around the northwest tip of this mesa. As you round the turn, notice the tall, rust-and-red sandstone walls and watch for windows into the sky. There are seven major arches from here to the end of the trail, along with numerous spires, giant alcoves, and contrasting desert patina. Notice how these canyons and their pinyon-juniper covered mesas all slope downward toward the Colorado River in the distance.

Miles and Directions

0.0 Sign in at trailhead.

0.5 Trail junction. Go left for 0.5 mile to First Arch overlook; go right to follow path to Rattlesnake Canyon Arches Trail.

0.7 Trail junction with Pollock Bench Trail. Go left to lower Rattlesnake Arches Trail.

3.0 End of trail beneath First Arch. Retrace steps.

6.0 Arrive back at trailhead.

19 Mee Canyon

With giant alcoves, windows, and spires, Mee Canyon offers one of the most exciting hikes in this high-desert country. While this is an easy route for experienced hikers, it is not recommended for inexperienced hikers because of the primitive nature of this trail. Directional signs and other evidence of human imprints are limited.

Distance: 5.6 miles out and back

Hiking time: 3 to 5 hours

Difficulty: Easy for experienced hikers; some scary sections along rock ledges, through a window, and down a ladder built into the side of the rock

Trail surface: Primitive, single-track backcountry trail marked intermittently with rock cairns. Some pathfinding skills are necessary.

Best season: Late April until the first snow flies (*Note:* Motorized travel is prohibited from Feb 15 to Apr 15.)

Other trail users: Foot traffic only

Canine compatibility: Allowed under control

Fees and permits: None

Maps: USGS Mack, Ruby Canyon, and Battleship Rock; Trails Illustrated Colorado National Monument/McInnis Canyons NCA

Trail contacts: BLM Grand Junction Field Office, 2815 H Rd., Grand Junction, CO 81506; (970) 244-3000, blm.gov/co/st/en/nca/mcnca.html

Special considerations: Moisture of any kind can make these roads impassable. Summer daytime temperatures can exceed 100 degrees Fahrenheit. This hike is best done early in the morning at this time of year. Water sources are limited and unreliable. Pack your own water. Biting gnats can be nasty from May through August. Pack insect repellant.

Finding the trailhead: Take I-70 west to exit 19, Fruita. Turn left on CO 340 and follow the signs to the Colorado National Monument. Turn right into the west entrance of the monument. Visitors headed to Glade Park or the McInnis Canyons National Conservation Area do not have to pay the entrance fee.

Travel 13.7 miles from the entrance station to the Glade Park Store turnoff sign located just past Upper Liberty Cap trailhead. Turn right and travel 0.2 mile to the Black Ridge Hunter Access Road. Turn right and stay on this road for 7.2 miles to the Mee Canyon Access Road. Turn left and travel 0.2 mile to the trailhead.

Two roads lead to this trailhead. Use of these roads is seasonally rotated for motorized travel. The upper road is open from April 15 to August 15, and the lower road from August 15 to February 15. No motorized travel is allowed on either road from February 15 to April 15. A high-clearance vehicle or four-wheel-drive vehicle is highly recommended. GPS: N39 05.7919' / W108 50.5826'

The Hike

There are parts of this hike that are scary—like the part where hikers inch their way across a narrow ledge of sandstone high above the canyon floor, or the part where they crawl through a tiny, narrow window arch on the edge of a massive alcove, then skinny down a Navajo-type ladder to the next narrow ledge leading to the bottom of this steep, yet fascinating gorge.

For adventurous hikers, however, this is one of the finest hikes on the upper Colorado River Plateau.

The trail begins with a gentle 1.3-mile decline across the top of the caprock Kayenta sandstone to the rim of Mee Canyon. From this point, hikers rapidly descend through the Entrada and Wingate sandstone layers to the canyon bottom.

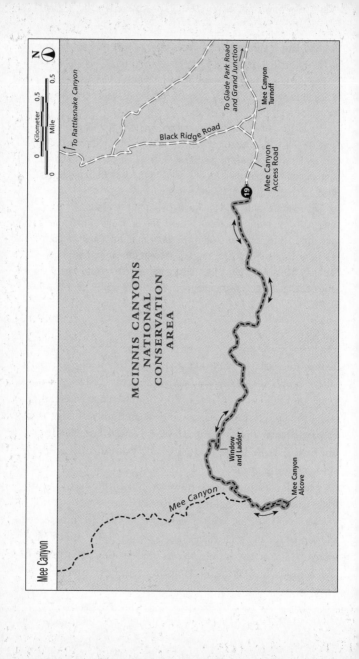

Mee Canyon

At 1.8 miles, hikers will be delighted to crawl through a window arch, then down a Navajo-style ladder, providing a great photo opportunity. The trail then crawls along the base of this large alcove, before dropping down a couple more benches in the sandstone layers. Just prior to reaching the bottom of the canyon, hikers will scoot across a narrow ledge of sandstone for about 30 feet. It looks scarier than it is.

Once in the bottom of the canyon at 2.5 miles, hikers continue upstream for another 0.3 mile to one of the largest alcoves in these canyonlands. Adventurous hikers can scramble upstream a little further, but the trail ends here. It's a good place for lunch in the shade before hiking back up and out.

Miles and Directions

0.0 Sign in at trailhead, then follow gentle decline to rim of Mee Canyon.

1.3 Drop down one bench into the canyon.

1.6 Drop down to the next bench.

1.7 Drop onto the third bench.

1.8 Crawl through a window arch, then climb down Navajo-style ladder. Follow curve of alcove to next bench down.

2.2 Drop around the corner of this alcove, then up, following rock cairns. Continue another 50 yards, then drop again. Careful. Loose rock.

2.5 Cross side creek and hike into bottom of canyon; begin upstream trek past first alcove.

2.8 Take right fork out of creek bottom and hike into Mee Canyon Alcove. Turn back and retrace steps.

5.6 Arrive back at trailhead.

BLM Rabbit Valley
(west of GJ)

20 McDonald Creek Cultural Area

There are four quality examples of ancient rock art in this canyon, although you will find only faint signs leading to their locations. As the BLM states, "it is hoped that visitors experience the canyon just as it was when Native Americans lived here, and to be an explorer feeling the excitement of discovering a remnant of your past."

Distance: 4.0 miles out and back
Hiking time: About 2 to 3 hours
Difficulty: Easy
Trail surface: Single-track, backcountry dirt trail, at times crossing creek bottom
Best season: Year-round, although can be blazing hot in midsummer
Other trail users: Foot and horseback traffic only
Canine compatibility: Dogs allowed under control; owners to pick up after their dogs
Fees and permits: None

Maps: USGS Colorado maps: Ruby Canyon, Mack, and Battleship Rock; USGS Utah map: Bitter Creek Well; Trails Illustrated Colorado National Monument/McInnis Canyons NCA
Trail contacts: BLM Grand Junction Field Office, 2815 H Rd., Grand Junction, CO 81506; (970) 244-3000, blm.gov/co/st/en/fo/gjfo.html
Special considerations: Pack insect repellant from May through August. Access road may be impassable when wet.

Finding the trailhead: Take I-70 west to exit 2, Rabbit Valley. Turn left (south) at the stop sign. Cross over the highway and in 0.2 mile enter McInnis Canyons NCA. Follow signs to McDonald Creek Cultural Area. In 0.6 mile, the road splits. Go left. (The road to the right leads to the campgrounds.) From here, the dirt road jumps into the streambed and follows it in and out for about 2 miles. Pass through the cattle guard at the Jouflas Horse Trail and enter the cultural area. In 3.3 miles, the road climbs out of the creek bed and in another 0.4 mile reaches the Castle Rocks Campground. Go left, downhill a couple hundred feet to the McDonald Creek Trailhead. A high-clearance vehicle is recommended for this road, which may be impassable when wet. GPS: N39 09.5139' / W 109 02.0386'

The Hike

BLM says, "As you search for sites and rock art, imagine where you might have found shelter from the elements if you were a Fremont Indian 1,000 years ago. Those places, such as cliff or rock overhangs, are the best places to look."

The first rock art panel is about 400 yards downstream from the parking area on the west-facing canyon wall. Look up about 15 feet and you will see red painted figures (pictographs).

There are four panels from the first one down to the mouth of McDonald Creek. Two of the panels are just below a drop-off (about 0.7 mile). On the east side of the canyon is a pecked panel (petroglyphs) and some historic names and dates, and on the west side is a painted panel. The last panel is high on the wall in a large alcove near the mouth of the creek.

Miles and Directions

0.0 Start from trailhead at northeast side of parking area; immediately cut across the streambed to the trail on the other side.

0.1 Pause and look around on the red rock face.

0.3 Cross the creek; trail will cross back and forth from here to the river, cutting the corners off most bends in the creek bed.

0.7 Large canyon enters from the left (Jouflas Horse Trail); cut to that side to hike around first big drop.

0.8 Climb down via rock stair steps.

1.8 Large alcove to your left. Look for pictographs.

2.0 Arrive at the railroad tracks and Colorado River. Knowles Canyon is across the river. Turn around and retrace steps.

4.0 Arrive back at trailhead.

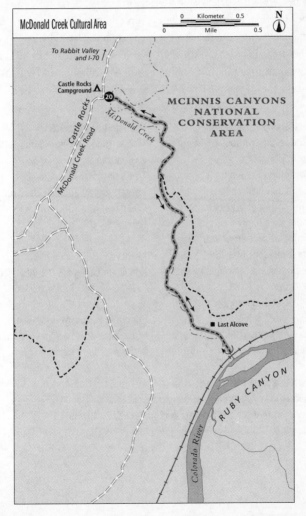

McDonald Creek Cultural Area

0 Kilometer 0.5

0 Mile 0.5

N

To Rabbit Valley and I-70

Castle Rocks Campground

20

McDonald Creek

MCINNIS CANYONS NATIONAL CONSERVATION AREA

Castle Rocks

McDonald Creek Road

■ Last Alcove

RUBY CANYON

Colorado River

21 Trail Through Time

This self-guided 1.5-mile loop trail could well have been this book's first, rather than twenty-first, entry, since it offers an excellent introduction to the geology and natural history of the area. From May through September, visitors can watch as paleontologists and volunteers meticulously search for fossils at the Mygatt-Moore Dinosaur Quarry.

Distance: 1.5-mile loop
Hiking time: About 45 minutes to 1.5 hours
Difficulty: Easy, although some parts mildly strenuous
Trail surface: Wheelchair accessible for a short way, turning to single-track, backcountry path
Best season: May through September when the dinosaur quarry is active
Other trail users: Foot traffic only, parts wheelchair accessible
Canine compatibility: Dogs allowed on leash

Fees and permits: None
Maps: None needed on this self-guided tour
Trail contacts: Museum of Western Colorado, 462 Ute Ave., Grand Junction, CO 81501; (970) 242-0971, museumof westernco.com. Also, BLM Grand Junction Field Office, 2815 H Rd., Grand Junction, CO 81506; (970) 244-3000, blm.gov/co/ st/en/fo/gjfo.html.
Special considerations: Take extra water as it can be very hot in the middle of summer.

Finding the trailhead: Take I-70 west toward Utah to exit 2, Rabbit Valley. At the top of the exit ramp, turn right and travel a few hundred feet toward the gate and trailhead. GPS: N39 11.6222' / W109 01.2053'

The Hike

This self-guided trail is operated through a cooperative agreement between the Museum of Western Colorado and the Bureau of Land Management. It is a well-maintained trail with fourteen interpretive stops. The trail dissects the Morrison geological formation that is well exposed here in Rabbit Valley. It takes visitors through that formation, climbing and falling 140 feet, with a general elevation of 4,700 feet above sea level.

It will take hikers a little longer to hike this trail than most 1.5-mile loop trails. That's because of all the time spent stopping and looking at the actual bones of long-dead dinosaurs and reading the interpretive signs. At one point, the x-shaped remnants of the neck vertebrae of a *Camarasaurus* skeleton (pronounced KAM-uh-ruh-SAW-rus) remain stuck in stone along the path. Sandstone channels along the Trail Through Time have preserved several individual dinosaurs virtually intact.

At another point, interpretive signs point to Utah's La Sal Mountains, 50 miles to the southwest, and discuss how they were formed and how the mighty Colorado River played its role in helping shape the landscape throughout this area.

The Mygatt-Moore quarry, discovered by Pete Mygatt and J. D. Moore in 1981, has turned out to be a fabulous fossil area. To date, eight different groupings of dinosaurs have been found here. It's famous for *Mymoorapelta*, a small armored dinosaur and the first *Ankylosaur* from the Jurassic period found in North America.

In fact, this is the site of many important fossil discoveries in the past thirty or so years, and scientific research continues. From May through September, visitors may watch as

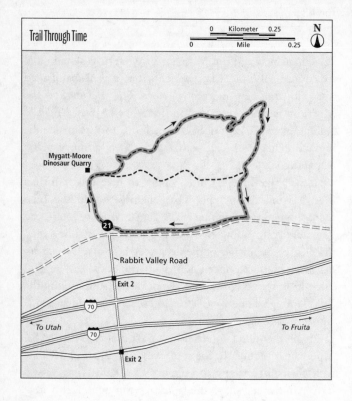

Trail Through Time

0 Kilometer 0.25

0 Mile 0.25

N

Mygatt-Moore
Dinosaur Quarry

21

Rabbit Valley Road

Exit 2

70

To Utah

70

To Fruita

Exit 2

paleontologists and volunteers meticulously search for fossils. If you'd like to join in, go to the Museum of Western Colorado's Dino Digs website at dinodigs.org/reservations .htm, and sign up for a summer dig.

Miles and Directions

0.0 Start at trailhead and interpretive signs at southwest corner of property.

0.1 First display.

0.1   Vault toilets to the left.

0.1   Kiosk at the quarry.

0.2   Trail wheelchair accessible to this point. Main trail splits; go left (uphill).

0.2   *Camarasaurus* skeleton.

0.4   Pass through gate. Close it behind you.

0.4   Shaded bench and Rabbit Valley overlook.

0.6   Drop to next level on hillside.

0.9   Vertebrae from back of *Diplodocus* preserved in sandstone ledge along the trail.

1.0   Last stop, explaining section/corner markers.

1.1   Travel through gate and onto frontage road. Turn right and hike back to the trailhead/vehicle.

1.5   Arrive back at trailhead.

BLM Book Cliffs Area
(northeast of GJ)

22 Coal Canyon

Coal Canyon is situated in the Little Book Cliffs Wild Horse Range, one of only three ranges in the United States set aside specifically to protect wild and free-roaming horses. The range encompasses 36,113 acres of rugged canyons and plateaus in the Book Cliffs, about 8 air miles north of Grand Junction.

Distance: 5.6 miles out and back

Hiking time: About 2 to 3 hours

Difficulty: Easy

Trail surface: 4WD jeep road

Best season: Winter and spring

Other trail users: Hikers and horseback riders only, Dec to May; ATVs, 4WDs, bikers also June to Nov

Canine compatibility: Dogs allowed under voice/leash control

Fees and permits: None

Maps: USGS Round Mountain and Cameo, Latitude 40° Fruita/Grand Junction; BLM Grand Junction

Trail contacts: BLM Grand Junction Field Office, 2815 H Rd., Grand Junction, CO 81506;

(970) 244-3000, blm.gov/co/st/en/fo/gjfo.html

Special considerations: Trails in the wild horse range are designed for foot and horse travel only. Motorized vehicles and mountain bikes are only allowed on the Coal Canyon Road from June 1 to Nov 30. Gates into Coal Canyon are closed to motorized vehicles from Dec 1 through May 30 to protect wintering wildlife and foaling areas.

Other: Friends of the Mustangs, a nonprofit group of volunteers, watches over the wild horses and advises the BLM on management (friendsofthemustangs .org).

Finding the trailhead: From Grand Junction, go east on I-70 to exit 45, Cameo. Turn left at the bottom of the exit, travel under the interstate, and then go right for 0.4 mile. Turn left, cross the river, and drive past the power plant, staying on the main road for approximately 1.8 miles to the Coal Canyon Trailhead and parking area. GPS: N39 09.7999' /W108 20.5359'

The Hike

From 90 to 150 wild horses roam the sagebrush parks and pinyon-juniper covered hills that dominate this area. Natural barriers such as cliffs and canyons, along with man-made fencing, help define the area and control horse movement. The 29,000-acre Little Book Cliffs Wilderness Study Area (WSA) makes up about two-thirds of the range.

The trail follows an old jeep road that's easier to hike than to drive. The road runs beneath or next to a power line—not a very pristine sight.

Hikers will soon forget about roads and power lines, however, when they spy a band (family) of wild horses. The horses move into this area during the winter because upper hillsides are covered in snow, and they stay through spring to have their young. Sightings are common at these times of year.

The hike begins on the road beneath the power line. A trail to the immediate right leads to Main Canyon. Continue forward (southwest). About every tenth of a mile, the road crosses the creek, eventually dropping into the normally dry creek bed at 1.5 miles.

Look for "stud piles," the first sign of horse activity. These large piles of manure are territorial markings left by rival males. Freshness of piles indicates how recently wild horses have been in the area.

Remember, wild horses are shy animals. Their instinct is to flee from danger. A stallion, however, can show aggression

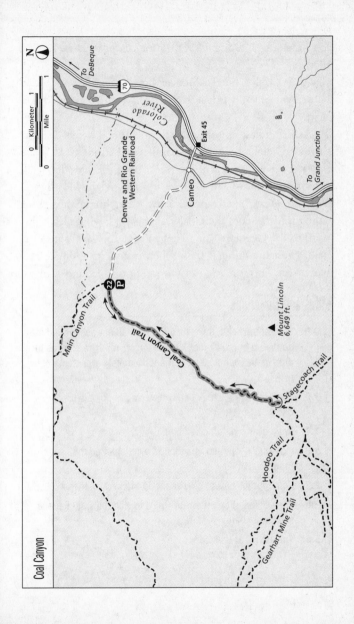

Coal Canyon

To DeBeque

Colorado River

Denver and Rio Grande
Western Railroad

Exit 45

Cameo

To Grand Junction

Main Canyon Trail

22
P

Coal Canyon Trail

Mount Lincoln
6,649 ft.

Stagecoach Trail

Hoodoo Trail

Gearhart Mine Trail

N

0   Kilometer   1

0   Mile   1

when he fears his family is being threatened. Enjoy viewing horses from a distance. Do not attempt to chase or feed them.

At 1.9 miles, hikers discover how Coal Canyon got its name. A coal seam to the right displays an abandoned coal shaft.

At 2.7 miles, visitors can see and touch a coal seam at shoulder height on the left-hand side of the road. At 2.8 miles, Coal Canyon Trail intersects with the Hoodoo Trail, which drops into Coal Canyon from the right (northwest). This strenuous hike leads to many other hiking/horseback riding trails, as does the Coal Canyon Trail, which leads forward to the Gearhart Mine Trail and the top of Mount Garfield. These are difficult trails when dry, virtually impassable when wet. This is a good turnaround point for most hikers.

Miles and Directions

0.0 Start at trailhead, traveling west, then southwest, around the north end of 6,649-foot Mount Lincoln; road/trail begins to drop in and out of creek bed approximately every tenth of a mile.

1.5 Road drops into creek bed, which by this point is usually dry.

1.7 Road climbs out of creek bed.

1.9 View coal seam and abandoned mine shaft on the right (northwest).

2.7 Road passes next to coal seam on the left (southeast).

2.8 Intersection of Coal Canyon Trail and Hoodoo Trail. Retrace steps from here.

5.6 Arrive back at trailhead.

Grand Mesa National Forest (east of GJ)

23 West Bench

The benches along the terraced Grand Mesa, the largest flattop mountain in the Northern Hemisphere, provide cool, shaded hikes during the heat of the summer in the valley below. Temperatures here are ten to twenty degrees cooler from May through September. The benches also are at a lower elevation than the top of the mesa, making them slightly easier for those not used to altitude. West Bench is the classic bench hike that takes trekkers to the top of Powderhorn Ski Area.

Distance: 6 miles out and back
Hiking time: About 2.5 hours
Difficulty: Easy to moderate if altitude is an issue
Trail surface: Wide, easy dirt trail into the forest, then single-track backcountry trail through forest, then volcanic rock fields; trail mostly relatively smooth and level
Best season: Late spring to early fall
Other trail users: No motorized traffic; some horseback/mountain bike use
Canine compatibility: Dogs allowed under control
Fees and permits: Day-use fee at self-serve fee station adjacent to Jumbo Campground, fisherman's parking area

Maps: USGS Skyway and Grand Mesa; USDA Forest Service Grand Mesa National Forest
Trail contacts: USDA Forest Service Office, 2777 Crossroads Blvd., Grand Junction, CO 81506; (970) 242-8211
Special considerations: Remember insect repellant; mosquitoes can get nasty here. While this trail is lower in elevation than the top of the mesa, the trailhead still sits at 9,926 feet. Altitude sickness here can still be a problem if visitors are not acclimated. If you feel light-headed or acquire a nasty headache, get to a lower elevation immediately. Carry extra water and hydrate often to help prevent altitude sickness. Always

remember you're in the Rockies, and weather can change
rapidly. Be prepared and dress
appropriately.

Finding the trailhead: Take I-70 east to exit 49, Powderhorn/Grand
Mesa. This is CO 65, a National Scenic Byway. Stay on it through the
town of Mesa and past Powderhorn Ski Area. Turn right toward the old
ranger station sign after passing Jumbo Reservoir. If you reach Mesa
Lakes Resort, you've gone about a tenth of a mile too far. Follow forest
service signs toward the old, now abandoned ranger station through
the Mesa Lakes group. Pay a day-use fee at the self-serve fee station,
and then continue to the right toward the fisherman's parking area and
trailhead. N39 03.1308' / W108 05.7072'

The Hike

This is an enjoyable, easy hike through aspen glades and
Engelmann spruce/Douglas fir forests, with loads of wildflowers in the summer; in the winter, it's a great cross-
country ski trail.

The hike begins by crossing a footbridge over the dam
to Sunset Lake, one of the many small ponds in the Mesa
Lakes group that also includes Jumbo Reservoir, Mesa Lake,
and Glacier Spring. The trail follows the top of the dike on
the northwest end of Sunset Lake for 0.2 mile before entering the forest. Private cabins have stood here as long as the
old ranger station on the north side of the creek, built by
the Civilian Conservation Corps in 1941. Please respect this
property. Part of the trail is on a private dirt road used to
access these cabins.

In 0.3 mile, West Bench Trail crosses Rim View Trail (No.
533). Continue forward and to the right. At 0.4 mile, West
Bench trail crosses Mesa Creek Trail (No. 505). Go left and
follow the signs along West Bench Trail. Within 0.1 mile, travel
between the final two cabins in this area and down the hill.

Hikers then wind their way along a bench of the mesa that lies in the transition zone between aspen and dark timber. It crosses a few minor volcanic rock fields as it continues slightly north and west until it winds into a lovely aspen forest with open meadows and lots of wildflowers at 1.3 miles. The trail continues to dart in and out of wooded areas and open meadows for another mile.

At 2.3 miles, hikers will cross a muddy creek where close observation shows elk and deer prints in the mud. At 2.4 miles, dark timber on the left and a thick aspen grove on the right frame a beautiful wildflower meadow frequented by numerous wildlife species.

In another 0.4 mile, the trail splits. To the right, hikers can see a hut and picnic table used by the ski patrol at the top of the Powderhorn Ski Area Lift No. 1. To the left, hikers may continue another 2.5 miles to Powderhorn Ski Area Lift No. 2. That, however, takes this a bit beyond an "easy day hike," adding another five miles to this six-mile out-and-back trek.

Go right to the picnic table, a nice place to snack and rest before the return trip.

Miles and Directions

0.0 At trailhead parking area, cross footbridge over Sunset Lake dam.

0.2 Go right, then follow signs to West Bench Trail, Powderhorn Ski Area Lifts Nos. 1 and 2.

0.3 Rim View Trail (No. 533) crosses West Bench Trail. Continue forward (right).

0.4 Trail connects to private road leading to cabins. In a few feet, it crosses Mesa Creek Trail (No. 505). Continue left and follow signs to West Bench Trail.

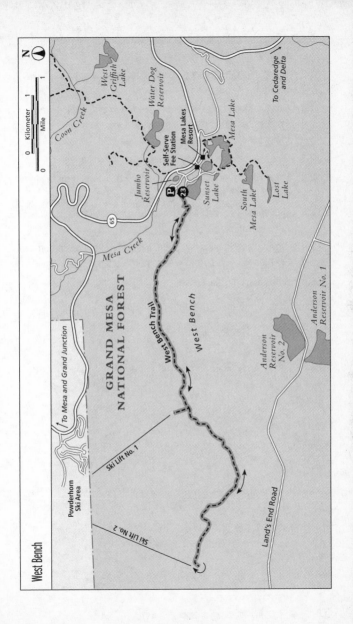

West Bench

0.5 Cross between last two cabins, leaving the private property behind.

1.3 Trail peeks out of dark timber into aspen and open meadows.

1.4 Original Mesa Creek Ski Area used to top out in this area. Excellent expert cross-country ski runs exist from here to the lower bench, approximately 1,000 feet below.

2.3 Cross muddy creek and look for signs of wildlife.

2.4 Large wildflower meadow framed with dark timber on the left and aspen on the right.

2.8 Trail splits. Go right to top of Lift No. 1; go left for 2.5 miles to top of Lift No. 2.

3.0 Arrive at picnic table/ski patrol hut and top of Powderhorn Ski Area Lift No. 1. Turn here to retrace steps.

6.0 Arrive back at trailhead.

24 Crag Crest

The Grand Mesa is the largest flattop mountain in the Northern Hemisphere, rising abruptly above valleys on the north, south, and west. Valley floors here lie between 4,500 and 5,500 feet in elevation. The top of the mesa varies from 10,000 to 11,000 feet above sea level, with the Crag Crest at its peak. Crag Crest Trail is a designated National Recreation Trail and is considered the signature hike on the Grand Mesa.

Distance: 10.4-mile loop (6.2-mile upper trail from east to west trailhead; 4.2-mile return on lower trail)

Hiking time: About 5 hours

Difficulty: Moderate (strenuous if altitude or distance are an issue!)

Trail surface: Backcountry trail with portions cutting through volcanic rock fields; upper section hard volcanic rock, dirt

Best season: Late spring to early fall

Other trail users: Hikers; horseback riders and bikers allowed between east trailhead and junction with Cottonwood Trail

Canine compatibility: Dogs allowed under control

Fees and permits: None

Maps: USGS Skyway and Grand Mesa; USDA Forest Service Grand Mesa National Forest

Trail contacts: USDA Forest Service Office, 2777 Crossroads Blvd., Grand Junction, CO 81506; (970) 242-8211.

Special considerations: This is a great trail to shuttle vehicles, with one vehicle parked at each trailhead. This shortens the hiking distance considerably. Take plenty of insect repellant, especially in the middle of the summer when mosquitoes can get nasty. Both trailheads are above 10,000 feet. The trail crests at 11,162 feet, about 2 miles above sea level! If you feel light-headed or acquire a nasty headache, get to a lower elevation immediately. Carry extra water and hydrate often to help prevent altitude sickness. Always remember you're in the Rockies, and weather can change rapidly. Be prepared, wear sturdy boots, and dress appropriately.

Finding the trailhead: *West trailhead:* Take I-70 east to exit 49, Powderhorn/Grand Mesa. This is CO 65, a National Scenic Byway. Stay on it for 34 miles, through the town of Mesa, past Powderhorn Ski Area, and past Mesa Lakes Resort. About 0.3 mile past Grand Mesa Lakes Lodge, turn left into the west Crag Crest Trailhead parking area near mile marker 28. *East trailhead:* The east trailhead is located at the Crag Crest Campground on FR 121 (Trickle Park Road). Continue on CO 65 past the west trailhead for approximately 1.0 mile. Turn left on FR 121 at the Grand Mesa visitor center. Follow this paved road for 2.5 miles. Turn left onto the gravel road and follow directional signs for another 0.9 mile to Eggleston Lake. The Crag Crest Trail parking area is on the right (south) side of the road. The trailhead is located past the campground on the left (northeast). GPS, east trailhead: N39 02.9306' / W107 56.2035'

The Hike

This route follows the loop from the east on the upper trail, returning on the lower trail, as it's best to hike the higher trail early in the day and avoid afternoon thunderstorms. Most of the elevation gain occurs within the first 2 miles, where hikers are met with spectacular views in all directions. This "Crag" crest is a long ridge left behind by two parallel glaciers in the last ice age. While the trail is not terribly difficult, other than an ascent on one end or the other, it is not suitable for hikers who fear heights. Along the crest, this trail narrows to about 3 feet wide with steep drops on both sides.

Also, this hike is shortened considerably by shuttling two vehicles, leaving one at each trailhead.

Watch the footing as jagged rocks grab ankles and stub toes along this trail. Good footgear is required. The upper trail traverses numerous black volcanic rock fields colored with green lichen and mosses and dotted with raspberry, red elderberry, blue gentian, and Colorado columbine. Scurrying about in these rock fields are great populations of picas and yellow-bellied marmots, lazing in the sun and eating wild flowers. At the 2.0-mile mark, hikers trek along the crest for about 2.0 miles before descending toward the lower trail. Great panoramic views are found all along this stretch. The San Juan Mountain Range is visible to the south. The West Elk Range spreads to the east. The Book Cliffs Range can be seen to the north. On most clear days, the La Sal Range in Utah can be seen to the west.

About a half mile before reaching the west trailhead, the trail splits. The lower trail proceeds to the left and returns to the east trailhead parking area. This lower trail flows through a lush forest with thick, tall grass and wildflowers and dense stands of aspen, Douglas fir, and Engelmann spruce, with large swaths of "blow down," where the dark timber was knocked down in a tremendous wind storm dozens of years ago.

Miles and Directions

0.0 Cross road from parking area to trailhead, 0.1 mile east, below the Crag Crest Campground.

0.1 Upper and lower trail splits. Go right to the upper trail.

1.1 Pass Bull Finch Reservoir No. 1; begin climb through volcanic rock field.

1.6 Pop out of dark timber and enjoy the views of the San Juan Mountains and Lone Cone Mountain, 125 miles to the south.

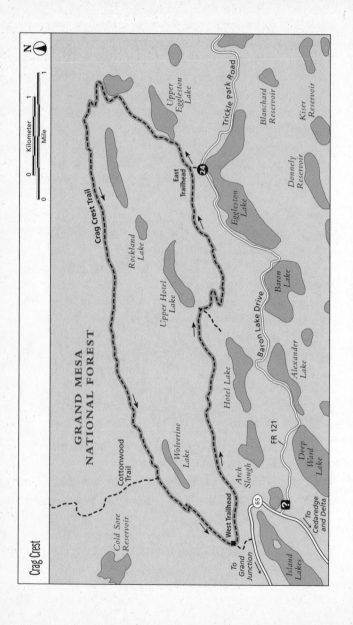

Crag Crest

GRAND MESA
NATIONAL FOREST

N

0   1   Kilometer
0   1   Mile

Cold Sore
Reservoir

Cottonwood
Trail

Crag Crest Trail

Upper
Eggleston
Lake

Trickle Park Road

Rockland
Lake

24

East
Trailhead

Upper Hotel
Lake

Eggleston
Lake

Blanchard
Reservoir

Kiser
Reservoir

Wolverine
Lake

Hotel Lake

Baron Lake Drive

Baron
Lake

Donnely
Reservoir

West Trailhead

Arch
Slough

FR 121

Alexander
Lake

To Grand
Junction

65

?

Deep
Ward
Lake

To
Cedaredge
and Delta

Island
Lakes

2.8 Ascend to 11,162 feet, the highest point along the crest.

3.5 Switchbacks lead down from top of the ridge; begin descent.

5.0 Junction with Cottonwood Trail (No. 712). Bicycles and horses not allowed past this point.

6.2 Junction of lower and upper trails. West trailhead is 0.5 mile to the right. Go forward and to the left along lower Crag Crest Trail.

6.3 Another trail intersection; go left via lower trail to east Crag Crest Trailhead.

7.7 Enjoy views from above Alexander Lakes Lodge and vicinity.

8.2 Cross creek, go right; climb through deadfall and continue back toward east trailhead.

10.2 Junction of upper and lower trails; go right to trailhead and parking area.

10.4 Arrive back at trailhead.

25 Lake of the Woods

A complex trail system provides numerous options for exploring Bull Basin, situated on a large bench on the northern flank of the Grand Mesa, the largest flattop mountain in the Northern Hemisphere. The Lake of the Woods Trail would be considered a typical trail on the mesa, as it flows through a lush forest with thick, tall grass and wildflowers, patches of low-growing Oregon grape, and dense stands of aspen, Douglas fir, and Engelmann spruce.

Distance: 5.3 miles out and back

Hiking time: About 2.5 to 3 hours

Difficulty: Easy to moderate

Trail surface: Backcountry trail through wet meadows, hard rock, dirt, slippery in spots when wet

Best season: Late spring to early fall

Other trail users: No motorized traffic; some horseback/mountain bike use, but trail mostly used by backpackers, backcountry anglers, and hunters during big game seasons (generally mid-Oct to mid-Nov)

Canine compatibility: Dogs allowed

Fees and permits: None

Maps: USGS Skyway and Grand Mesa; USDA Forest Service Grand Mesa National Forest

Trail contacts: USDA Forest Service Office, 2777 Crossroads Blvd., Grand Junction, CO 81506; (970) 242-8211

Special considerations: Take plenty of insect repellant, especially in the middle of the summer, when the mosquitoes can get nasty. Trail elevation ranges from 9,971 to 10,176 feet—nearly 2 miles above sea level. If you feel light-headed or acquire a nasty headache, get to a lower elevation immediately. Always carry extra water and hydrate often to help prevent altitude sickness. Always remember you're in the Rockies, and weather can change rapidly. Be prepared and dress appropriately.

Finding the trailhead: Travel east from Grand Junction on I-70 for 20 miles to exit 49, Grand Mesa/Powderhorn. That's CO 65, a National Scenic and Historic Byway.

Go through the town of Mesa, past Powderhorn Ski Area, and into the Grand Mesa National Forest. About 2 miles past the Mesa Lakes Resort area, on the last long curve before heading up the final stretch to the top of the Grand Mesa, you'll come to mile marker 38. Beyond the mile marker is a long cabled guard rail. Just past the cabled guard rail, turn left on graveled FR 250. (This forest service road is not marked.) Travel 0.4 mile to a parking area large enough for horse trailers. The road ends here. GPS: N39 06.2219' / W108 04.6272'

The Hike

The trailhead for Lake of the Woods is almost 10,200 feet above sea level. (Lake of the Woods Trail actually gives up a couple hundred feet of elevation from the trailhead, but climbs again.)

This particular trail is designed for foot and horseback traffic. Motorized vehicles are not allowed, unless you work for the Bull Creek Reservoir Company, which owns the reservoirs on this bench and utilizes ATVs to monitor the reservoirs.

About 1.5 miles from the trailhead, you'll come to a misspelled sign at the junction of Lake of the Woods Trail 506, and Bull Creek "Cutofe" Trail 506-1A. If you take the Bull Creek Cutoff, you'll wind your way over to Bull Creek Reservoir No. 4, and eventually to the road that leads past Waterdog Reservoir and back to CO 65 across from Jumbo Reservoir in the Mesa Lakes group.

If you stick to the Lake of the Woods trail, however, you'll generally follow the ridge line of the Crag Crest to

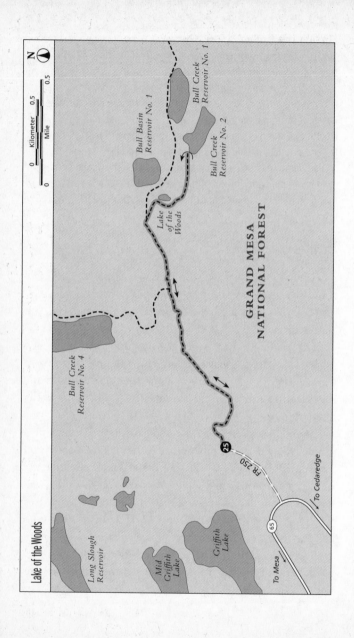

Lake of the Woods

GRAND MESA
NATIONAL FOREST

Bull Creek Reservoir No. 1

Bull Basin Reservoir No. 1

Bull Creek Reservoir No. 2

Lake of the Woods

Bull Creek Reservoir No. 4

Long Slough Reservoir

Mid Griffith Lake

Griffith Lake

25

FR 250

To Cedaredge

To Mesa

65

0   Kilometer   0.5

0   0.5   Mile

N

Bull Basin. (Crag Crest is the famous top ridge line of the Grand Mesa that runs parallel to this trail. This "Crag" crest is a long rocky ridge left behind by two parallel glaciers in the last ice age. It's about 6 miles long and reaches an elevation of 11,160 feet.) In about 10 minutes, you'll discover a few other trail junctions, but stick to the right, or toward the ridge line, and you'll pop up to Lake of the Woods—a tiny pond and not really a lake at all).

Continuing on the trail to the north and east of this small pond, you'll find Bull Creek Reservoir No. 1. If you continue on the trail to the south of Lake of the Woods, you'll head to Bull Creek Reservoir No. 2. This, Bull Basin Reservoir No. 1, and Bull Creek Reservoir No. 1 are all about the same size, approximately 10 acres and 10 to 12 feet deep, although the water level fluctuates greatly with irrigation demand.

No developed campsites exist at these reservoirs, so you must pack out what you pack in. (Note to anglers: Fishing here is by artificial flies only. The bag, possession, and size limit for trout is two fish, 16 inches or longer.)

The trail gets a little more rugged from here, but you can continue on Lake of the Woods Trail all the way to Cottonwood Lake about 2 miles further to the northeast.

Miles and Directions

0.0 Start from trailhead and parking area.

0.3 Veer to your left around the marshy meadow in front of you.

1.5 Intersection with Bull Creek Cutoff.

2.6 Arrive at Bull Creek Reservoir No. 2. Retrace steps from here.

5.3 Arrive back at trailhead.

Colorado River (through the center of the Grand Valley)

26 Colorado Riverfront Trail

This paved trail parallels the Colorado River for 28.5 miles through the Grand Valley, from Palisade to Fruita. The newest 8.5-mile section of the Colorado Riverfront Trail was opened in September 2014. All but 4.3 miles is now a wheelchair-accessible biking/walking/jogging/in-line-skating/mom-with-stroller/dog-walking path. Users can pick and choose the section or sections they'd like to visit as access points are numerous throughout the valley.

Distance: 28.5 miles from Palisade to Fruita; including spur trails, total paved length more than 33 miles

Hiking time (Times listed are one way. Double that if you have to retrieve your vehicle.): Palisade/Riverbend Park section, 1.8 miles one way, approx. walking time 40 minutes; 33½ Road to Corn Lake (Clifton Nature Park section), 1.5 miles one way, approx. walking time 30 minutes; Corn Lake to 29 Road (Parks and Wildlife section), 3 miles one way, approx. walking time 1 hour; 29 Road to 27½ Road (bicycles only on the roadway; no pedestrian traffic); 27½ Road to Western Colorado Botanical Gardens (Los Colonias section), 1.5 miles one way, approx. walking time 30 minutes; Western Colorado Botanical Gardens to Broadway and West Avenue (Riverside section), 1.5 miles one way, approx. walking time 30 minutes; Broadway and West Avenue to 24 Road (Blue Heron section), 3 miles one way, approx. hiking time 1 hour; 24 Road to Walker State Wildlife Area, 2 miles one way, approx. hiking time 40 minutes; Walker State Wildlife Area to Heritage Park in Fruita, 8.5 miles one way, approx. hiking time 3 hours

Difficulty: Easy

Trail surface: Paved path, 8 to 12 feet wide

Best season: Year-round; great along the river during summer heat

Other trail users: Foot and bicycle traffic; no motorized vehicles

Canine compatibility: Dogs allowed on leash; owners to pick up after pets

Fees and permits: None

Maps: USGS Latitude 40° Fruita/Grand Junction; free downloadable section maps also available from riverfrontproject .org

Trail contacts: Colorado Riverfront Commission, 544 Rood Ave., P.O. Box 2477, Grand Junction, CO 81502; (970) 683-4333, info@riverfrontproject.org

Special considerations: While most of this trail is a dedicated pathway for foot and bicycle traffic only, there are 4.3 miles of trail yet to be built. In those places, the current path runs along roads from 36¼ Road to 33½ Road and from 29 Road to 27½ Road. While these roads provide continuous passage through the valley for bicyclists, they are not safe for walkers/hikers.

Finding the trailhead: In Palisade, go to Riverbend Park. For parking along the hike or for those joining the hike farther to the west, use the following sites: In Clifton, go to James Robb Colorado River State Park at Corn Lake on 32 Road. In Grand Junction, find parking at Western Colorado Botanical Gardens at Seventh Street and Struthers; Riverside parking area at Broadway and West Avenues; Junior Service League Park at the Colorado River and Redlands Parkway, aka 24 Road; or Walker State Wildlife Area on Railhead Boulevard and the River Road. If walking the trail east to west from Fruita, park at the Colorado Welcome Center, or Heritage Park on the South Frontage Road. GPS at Riverbend Park in Palisade: N39 10.0562' / W108 37.2311'; GPS at Heritage Park in Fruita: N39 15.2225' / W108 73.1072'

The Hike

There are numerous starting/ending spots for this trail for walkers, bicyclists, and other self-propelled outdoor enthusiasts.

Visitors can reach the Palisade section of Riverfront Trail at the town's Riverbend Park, which features covered picnic shelters, eighteen holes of disc golf, two large pavilions, a stocked fishing pond, boat launch to the Colorado River, playground, and barbeque facilities. This paved stretch is 1.8 miles long. At the west end of the park, the trail spills onto the roadway. Bicycles can continue for 2.8 miles on the roadway to 33½ Road, before the paved section of the riverfront trail begins again. Hikers must return to their vehicles and drive to the next best parking area along the trip at the James Robb Colorado River State Park/Corn Lake section, on 32 Road in Clifton.

The stretch of trail between 33½ Road and Corn Lake is called the Clifton Nature Park section and is one of the most scenic parts of trail, traveling through a stretch of lovely cottonwood trees along the north bank of the river.

The trail continues on a path under 32 Road before entering the state park at Corn Lake. Turn right, walk through the parking lot at the east end of the lake, then turn left between park headquarters and the lake, walking downstream past the vault toilets. The trail travels past the west end of Corn Lake and onto the Parks and Wildlife section of trail. It meanders through a stretch of old gravel pits, now used as fishing ponds, to 29 Road. Watch for osprey and great blue herons. Here, again, the trail stops on the road. Walkers must return to their vehicles, while bicyclists turn right on 29 Road, pedal 0.3 mile to C½ Road, and turn left. Be careful. The speed limit on 29 Road is 45 mph!

The bicycle trail continues along C½ Road for 1.5 miles. C½ Road ends at a sharp right turn on 27½ Road. The Riverfront Trail exits the roadway here and continues forward, to the west. Walkers back in their vehicles can find new parking adjacent to the Western Colorado Botanical Gardens to enjoy this stretch, called the Las Colonias section. The Riverfront Trail is paved and separated from all roads for the remainder of the trip to Fruita, another 13 miles.

It travels past the botanical gardens, where one of the first spur trails was built on Watson Island. The island, the botanical gardens, and the quaint outdoor amphitheater that sits between the two were once the site of the largest dumping ground in the valley, which was piled with junk cars, rotting barrels of ooze, and old refrigerators. This is where the dream of a riverfront trail first took shape.

The trail travels under the Fifth Street bridge and the old black railroad bridge, then onto the Riverside section of the trail. For hikers just entering the trail, a good parking area sits at the southwest corner of Broadway and West Avenue. This lot leads to the Blue Heron section of the Riverfront Trail. Spur trails from here lead to the James Robb Colorado River State Park Connected Lakes section and the Audubon Trail, also leading into the park.

The Blue Heron section leads to the Junior Service League Park at 24 Road/Redlands Parkway, where outhouses are available. From here, the trail travels along the river, then under the Redlands Parkway on the way to Walker State Wildlife Area at Railhead Avenue. Another large parking facility is available here for the final stretch into Fruita, now known as the Monument View section. Be cautious in the last few miles, as the trail crosses a number of driveways along South Frontage Road all the way to the Colorado Welcome Center, 8.5 miles from the wildlife area.

Miles and Directions

0.0 From parking area in Riverbend Park (N39 10.0562' / W108 37.2311') head west on paved Riverfront Trail for 1.8 miles where paved trail ends on gravel/dirt parking area leading to 36¼ Road (N39 10.0290' / W108 37.8352'). Walkers must return to Riverbend Park.

1.8 Bicyclists may continue for 2.8 miles along roadways to 33½ Road where the paved Riverfront Trail begins again. (N39 06.9950' / W108 43.1609'). There is no parking at this spot.

6.7 Next parking area located on D Road between 32¼ and 32½ roads (N39 06.2665' / W108 45.2186'). Dedicated, paved trail spur winds east, then south for 0.3 mile and connects to main Riverfront Trail system. Walkers can turn left and travel 1.4 miles northeast, or they may turn right and travel 0.7 mile to the 32 Road underpass and Colorado River State Park, Corn Lake section (N39 05.5380' / W108 46.0426'). Another parking lot is available here, but visitors must pay the state parks pass fee of $7.

7.7 Frum the underpass, travel north, then west around Corn Lake for approximately 1 mile, then begin a 3-mile trek through the Parks and Wildlife section to 29 Road where the trail ends for walkers (N39 05.1976' / W108 51.5029').

11.7 Bicyclists may continue right (north) on 29 Road to C½ Road and turn left. Use caution here. Speed limit for vehicles is 45 mph. Continue on C½ Road to 27½ Road. Turn left onto paved, dedicated Riverfront Trail.

13.7 From 27½ Road to Fruita, the Riverfront Trail is now complete, with no interruptions. The next best access point is at the Western Colorado Botanical Gardens, South 7th Street and Struthers Avenue. A spur trail leads from the parking area just east of the botanical gardens to the main Riverfront Trail (N39 05.4737' / W108 56.0603'). From here, you can walk east for 1.2 miles to 27½ Road, or travel west

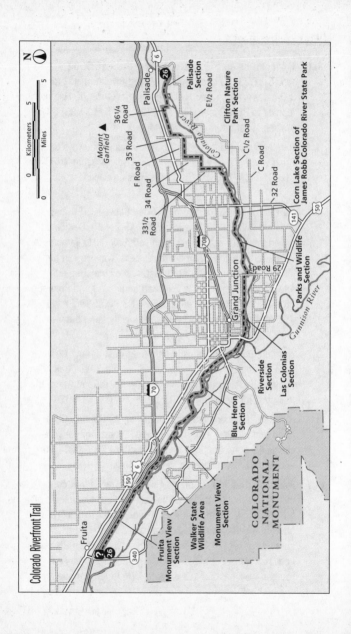

Colorado Riverfront Trail

1.7 miles to Broadway and West Avenue and the Blue Heron Section (N39 06.7405' / W108 58.0145').

16.6 From the parking area on the southwest corner of Broadway and West Avenue, walkers can hike east back toward the botanical gardens, or continue traveling downriver beneath the Broadway underpass and northwest for 1.2 miles to a parking area near the Riverside Parkway and Banana's Fun Park (N39 08.1822' / W108 59.1969').

17.8 Continue 2.1 miles west on the north side of the Colorado River to 24 Road at Junior Service League Park (N39 08.9270' / W108 61.1840'). Adequate parking is available throughout this area.

19.9 Follow trail between 24 Road and the Colorado River for approximately 0.6 mile. The trail will then travel underneath the 24 Road bridge and continue for 2.3 miles to Walker State Wildlife Area at Railhead Avenue (N39 10.6291' / W108 64.9753'). Parking is available here.

22.8 Travel northwest 5.8 miles from the state wildlife area to Heritage Park in Fruita (N39 15.2225' / W108 73.1072').

28.5 Arrive at Heritage Park. (Additional miles can be found on spur trails all throughout the valley.)

Appendix: Groups and Organizations

Colorado Canyons Association (CCA), 543 Main St., Suite 4, Grand Junction, CO 81501; coloradocanyonsassociation.org

Colorado National Monument Association (CNMA), 1750 Rim Rock Dr., Fruita, CO 81521; coloradonma.org

Colorado Riverfront Commission, 544 Rood Ave., P.O. Box 2477, Grand Junction, CO 81502; (970) 683-4333, info@riverfrontproject.org

Dinosaur Journey Museum (operated by Museum of Western Colorado), 550 Jurassic Ct., Fruita, CO 81521; (970) 858-7282, museumofwesternco.com

Friends of the Mustangs, friendsofthemustangs.org

Museum of Western Colorado, 462 Ute Ave., Grand Junction, CO 81501; (970) 242-0971, museumofwesternco.com

About the Author

Bill Haggerty was born and raised in Colorado with a love of the outdoors. He and his brothers would follow their father, Bill Sr., along the front range of the Rockies, especially the small creeks and streams around Estes Park, where they hiked and fished and camped throughout their childhoods.

Bill Jr. graduated from the University of Colorado School of Journalism in 1976 and moved to the West Slope of Colorado, where he worked for local newspapers. He covered cops, courts, and high school sports but wrote about the magnificent, wild environs of Western Colorado.

His love of writing and the great outdoors took him to the Colorado Division of Wildlife, where he spent twenty-plus years as its information/education specialist in the Grand Junction area. For eighteen of those years, he produced a weekly outdoors and wildlife television series called *Bill's Backyard*. He also helped write, promote, and teach Project WILD, a program for K-12 educators that incorporated wildlife concepts into school curriculums.

A joint project of the Western Association of Fish and Wildlife Agencies and the Western Regional Environmental Education Council, Project WILD's goal was "to assist learners of all ages in developing awareness, knowledge, skills, and commitment to result in informed decisions, responsible behavior, and constructive actions concerning wildlife and the environment upon which all life depends."

Haggerty continues to believe in that goal, and he continues to educate. Since 2003, he has written a weekly outdoor column for the *Grand Junction Daily Sentinel*, featuring some of the hikes found in this guide.

Haggerty and his wife, Glenda, raised two children, Bridgette and Austin, who have moved on to their own wild places. He and Glenda continue to reside in Grand Junction with their Norwegian Elkhounds, who hike with them often—when they're not in the national monument (no dogs allowed there!).